D0205173

YOSEMITE & NEIGHBORING PARKS

9th Edition

NO LONGER PROPERTY OF
SEATTLE PUBLIC LIBRARY

By Rosemary McClure
& Jim Edwards

Climbing Moro Rock, Sequoia National Park.
PREVIOUS PAGE: **An iconic view of Yosemite Valley.**

FROMMER'S STAR RATINGS SYSTEM

Every hotel, restaurant, and attraction listed in this guide has been ranked for quality and value. Here's what the stars mean:

★ Recommended
★★ Highly Recommended
★★★ A must! Don't miss!

AN IMPORTANT NOTE

The world is a dynamic place. Hotels change ownership, restaurants hike their prices, museums alter their opening hours, and buses and trains change their routings. And all of this can occur in the several months after our authors have visited, inspected, and written about these hotels, restaurants, museums, and transportation services. Though we have made valiant efforts to keep all our information fresh and up-to-date, some few changes can inevitably occur in the periods before a revised edition of this guidebook is published. So please bear with us if a tiny number of the details in this book have changed. Please also note that we have no responsibility or liability for any inaccuracy or errors or omissions, or for inconvenience, loss, damage, or expenses suffered by anyone as a result of assertions in this guide.

CONTENTS

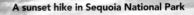

A sunset hike in Sequoia National Park

A LOOK AT YOSEMITE AND SEQUOIA & KINGS CANYON NATIONAL PARKS

Half Dome. El Capitan. Trees so big you can drive a car through them. Crashing waterfalls, meadows full of wildflowers, and dense forests that span endless miles: Yosemite and Sequoia & Kings Canyon national parks are an archetypal part of the American identity and as iconic as the Statue of Liberty or the Golden Gate Bridge. And a trip through the parks—whether by car, RV, park shuttle, or on foot or bike—is as epic as the parks themselves. Whether your goal is to find solitude on a backcountry hike, feel the mist of a waterfall on your face, or snap photos of the parks' abundant wildlife, there's an experience waiting for you amid these mighty peaks and valleys. What follows is just a brief look at many of the wonders you'll encounter. *Happy trails!*

A hiker sits on a fallen giant sequoia tree in Grant's Grove, Sequoia National Park.

The trail to Upper Yosemite Fall is strenuous, but intrepid hikers are rewarded with heart-stopping views of Yosemite Valley. Read more about day and overnight Yosemite hikes in chapter 4.

Tunnel View (p. 32) under a full moon. This observation area provides one of the park's most recognizable vistas, famously captured on film by photographer Ansel Adams.

The Mist Trail is so named because the spray from the fall drenches anyone who tackles this route, especially in spring. See p. 44.

Set in a bowl of granite surrounded by sheer slopes, Tenaya Lake (p. 54) offers canoeing, hiking, fishing, sailing, and even swimming—for those who don't mind the chilly water.

Hikers en route to the Hetch Hetchy Reservoir. Though passionately opposed by conservationist John Muir and reviled by environmentalists to this day, the reservoir provides drinking water to San Francisco.

Half Dome (p. 43) at sunset, reflected in the Merced River, which winds through the length of Yosemite Valley.

Nevada Fall is reached by hiking along a portion of the 211-mile John Muir Trail (p. 59).

Cross country skiers at Glacier Point. The park has more than 350 miles of skiable trails and roads, including 25 miles of machine-groomed track and 90 miles of marked trails. See p. 61 for more on skiing in the park.

The moderately strenuous hike to Cathedral Lakes (p. 48) has a 1,000-foot elevation gain, rewarded by views of the surrounding peaks and domes reflected in the glass-like water.

A hiker pauses in a meadow, with Bridalveil Fall in the distance. A paved path leads to the base of the fall (see p. 42), which is at its peak flow in spring and early summer.

Steller's jays, recognizable by their bright blue body, dark head, and prominent crest, are unfazed by humans and are likely to show up anywhere near food.

Often confused with the much larger and more aggressive grizzly bear, the black bear is the largest mammal in the park. With so many around, secure food storage is a must for campers.

Named for their large, mule-like ears, mule deer are most frequently seen grazing in meadows at dawn and dusk.

Tenaya Lodge at Yosemite (p. 74) is set on 48 acres surrounded by Sierra National Forest, and offers hotel rooms, cottages, and cabins, plus year-round recreational activities.

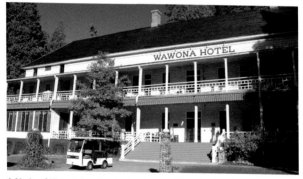

A National Historic Landmark, the Wawona Hotel (p. 68) is built in classic Victorian style, and set near towering trees in an expansive green clearing. The main building was constructed in 1879.

The historic Ahwahnee Hotel (p. 65) has hosted Queen Elizabeth II and President John F. Kennedy, and offers stellar views from nearly every window.

SEQUOIA

Giant sequoias (p. 151) are the world's largest trees, able to live 3,000 years. Many grow as tall as a 26-story building.

On a clear day, the views from the Moro Rock lookout stretch for miles (p. 103).

Many day hikes in Sequoia are suitable for casual hikers, and allow them to see a unique landscape created over the course of millions of years.

The drive-through Tunnel Log is a stop along Moro Rock/Crescent Meadow Road, a short, scenic drive in Sequoia National Park (see p. 108).

Crystal Cave (p. 105), formed from limestone that turned to marble, contains an array of cave formations, many still growing.

Ranger programs in Sequoia include weekend wildflower walks, talks about park history, and evening campfire programs.

The General Sherman Tree (p. 96), is believed to be about 2,100 years old—and it's still growing.

Yellow-bellied marmots live in the park's higher elevations and like to munch on car hoses and wiring. Check under the hood before you drive off.

Parts of Kings Canyon Highway offer motorists a close-up view of the Kings River, which crashes over and among huge boulders. Pictured here is the spectacular Grizzly Falls (p. 108).

Plan a stop at the Giant Forest Museum (p. 94) to learn about the park's star attractions, the giant sequoias, as well as human history in the park.

Recreation options at family-friendly Montecito Sequoia Lodge (p. 130) include horseback riding, as well as fishing, cross-country skiing, sailing, and canoeing.

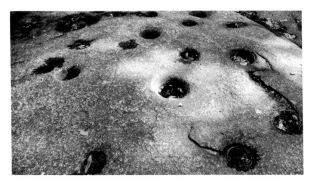

The easy Potwisha and River's Edge hike (p. 120) leads to the site of what was once a thriving Native American village, including a bedrock area with mortar holes where women ground acorns into meal.

KINGS CANYON

Accessed by overnight hike or an ambitious one-day hike, Kings Canyon's Paradise Valley (p. 118) is sprawling, relatively flat, and absolutely beautiful.

Spring and early summer are the best times to appreciate the park's many rivers, fed by melting snow at higher elevations.

Wilderness and solitude in Kings Canyon are never very far away—just about any hike that lasts more than an hour will get you into the wild.

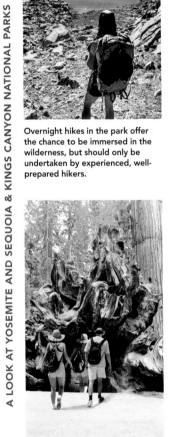

Overnight hikes in the park offer the chance to be immersed in the wilderness, but should only be undertaken by experienced, well-prepared hikers.

The park doesn't have many gas stations, so fill up when you see one.

The General Grant Tree Trail is an interpretive walk explaining the role forest fires play in the park's life cycle.

A patch of Sierra Shooting Star wildflowers, one of the many varieties found in spring and summer in the parks.

THE BEST OF YOSEMITE AND SEQUOIA & KINGS CANYON NATIONAL PARKS

It's no secret: We love national parks, especially Yosemite, which ranks as one of the nation's top five in popularity—and with good reason. With its mind-boggling rock formations and astonishing waterfalls, Yosemite is one of the wonders of the natural world. It is—or should be—on everyone's must-see list, along with Sequoia's colossal trees and King Canyon's jaw-dropping backcountry. All three of these amazing national parks owe their existence to the geological and glacial forces that formed the Sierra Nevada mountain range, which stretches more than 400 miles across California's Central Valley. Together the parks cover 1.6 million acres, host more than 5½ million visitors a year, and are home to thousands of species of plants and animals.

Although Yosemite National Park wasn't the first national park, the idea was born here. In 1864, Abraham Lincoln set aside the Yosemite Valley and the Mariposa Grove of giant sequoias as a California state park—the first time the federal

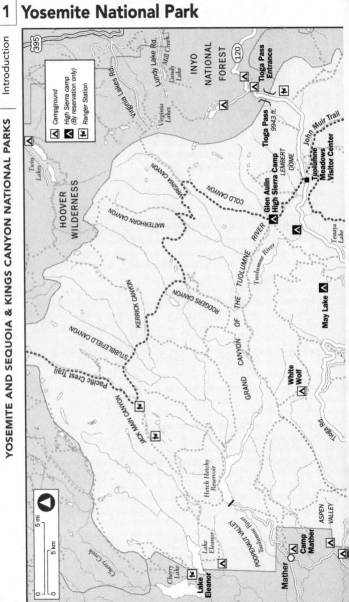

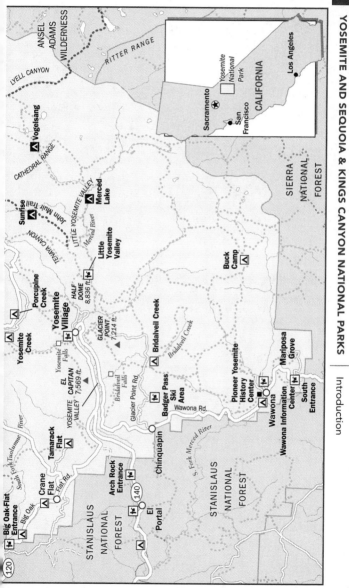

1 | Sequoia & Kings Canyon National Parks

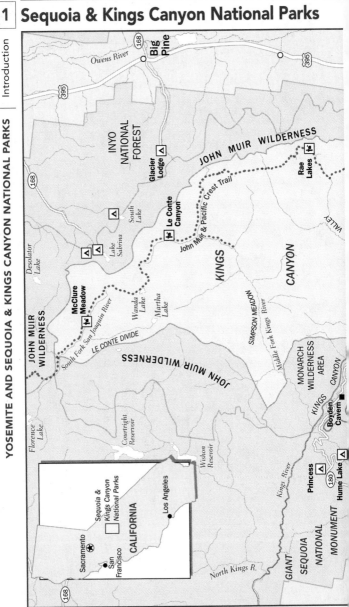

4

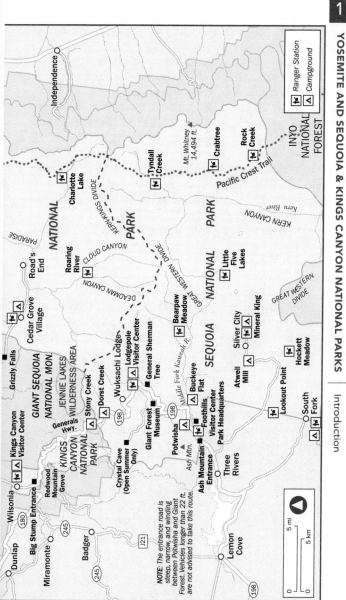

Ranger Station
Campground

Independence

INYO NATIONAL FOREST

Mt. Whitney 14,494 ft.

Crabtree

Rock Creek

Tyndall Creek

Pacific Crest Trail

Charlotte Lake

KERN/KINGS DIVIDE

PARADISE

NATIONAL

CLOUD CANYON

Roaring River

Road's End

DEADMAN CANYON

GREAT WESTERN DIVIDE

Kern River

KERN CANYON

PARK

Little Five Lakes

NATIONAL

Cedar Grove Village

PARK

Bearpaw Meadow

Wuksachi Lodge

Lodgepole Visitor Center

General Sherman Tree

Middle Fork Kaweah R.

Silver City

Mineral King

GREAT WESTERN DIVIDE

Grizzly Falls

GIANT SEQUOIA NATIONAL MON.

JENNIE LAKES WILDERNESS AREA

Stony Creek

Dorst Creek

198

Buckeye

Hockett Meadow

SEQUOIA

Kings Canyon Visitor Center

Generals Hwy.

Giant Forest Museum

198

Atwell Mill

Foothills Visitor Center

Lookout Point

NATIONAL

Redwood Mountain Grove

KINGS CANYON NATIONAL PARK

Crystal Cave (Open Summer Only)

Potwisha

Ash Mtn.

Park Headquarters

South Fork

Wilsonia

180

Big Stump Entrance

Ash Mountain Entrance

Three Rivers

Dunlap

245

Miramonte

Badger

245

J21

Lemon Cove

198

NOTE: The entrance road is steep, narrow, and winding between Potwisha and Giant Forest. Vehicles longer than 22 ft. are not advised to take this route.

5 mi

5 km

government designated land for preservation in such a manner. Yellowstone became the world's first national park eight years later. In 1890, Yosemite and Sequoia followed suit, followed by King's Canyon in 1940.

Travelers cherish these parks—particularly Yosemite—and visit in record numbers, stretching resources and infrastructure beyond what was ever intended.

Roughly the size of Rhode Island, Yosemite receives more than 4 million visitors annually. Almost everyone crowds into 7-mile-long Yosemite Valley, which attracts 95% of all visitors, even though it is just 1% of the park by area. Here visitors find the park's most famous landmarks—Half Dome and El Capitan—as well as the highest waterfall in North America and three of the tallest in the world (Upper Yosemite, Sentinel, and Ribbon falls).

"We realize that for a lot of people, this is their one and only trip to the park," said Yosemite spokesman Scott Gediman. "It's incumbent upon us to protect that experience as much as we can."

But it is also incumbent upon visitors to avoid the park on busy summer days, if possible. Or at least arrive very early. The alternative could be a 2-hour traffic standstill trying to get into the park—or worse, the inability to find a parking place when you do.

While Sequoia & Kings Canyon national parks also are busy in the summer, the crowds are more manageable. The parks are adjacent to each other about 70 miles south of Yosemite and are home to both the largest giant sequoia trees in the world and a deep canyon that rivals Yosemite Valley for awe-inspiring beauty. Their peaks stretch across 1,350 square miles and include 14,505-foot Mount Whitney, the tallest point in the lower 48 states. Three powerful rivers, the Kings, Kern, and Kaweah, tumble through them. Despite their large size, Sequoia & Kings Canyon National Parks attract less than half the number of Yosemite's annual visitors, making them a great alternative for those looking to avoid huge crowds.

THE best OF YOSEMITE AND SEQUOIA & KINGS CANYON

It's hard to pick the best of anything in Yosemite, Sequoia, or Kings Canyon. There are so many splendid hikes, roaring waterfalls, and mind-blowing vistas to see. But here are a few suggestions.

The Best Views

o **The Panorama from Tunnel View Outside Yosemite Valley:** Traveling toward Yosemite Valley from the West on CA 41, the Wawona Tunnel provides one of the world's great reveals of natural scenery. Luckily there's a parking lot nearby. El Capitan, Half Dome, Bridalveil Fall—it's all there for you to soak in. See p. 32.

Photo Tip: For the best light, come back an hour before sunset. It will be behind you as you view the valley; keep shooting as the sun disappears. The result might be a wall-worthy print.

o **Moro Rock in Sequoia National Park:** A hike of 400 steps up this massive granite boulder is worth the effort. Handrails help. The views can be spectacular, allowing you to gaze as far as the eye can see. See p. 103.

Photo Tip: If you have a camera or smartphone that allows you to shoot panoramas, here's a great place to test it out. If it's not crowded, you could literally capture a 360-degree image.

o **The General Grant Tree in Kings Canyon:** A short hike brings you to the second largest tree in the world. It's difficult to fathom its immensity, even when you're standing in front of it. See p. 114.

Photo Tip: How do you eat an elephant? One bite at a time, according to the old joke. That's exactly what you need to do when trying to shoot this tree. At first, aim your lens at close-ups: the bark, the base. Spend time viewing it from all angles, appreciate where the light hits. Then move back. Look for ways to shoot it among the smaller trees and with people to give it scale.

The Best Car Campgrounds

o **North Pines Campground in Yosemite Valley:** Smaller and slightly more isolated than neighboring campgrounds, North Pines offers a true forest camping experience that makes it the most enjoyable of Yosemite Valley's car campgrounds. See p. 77.

o **Buckeye Flat Campground in Sequoia:** This is a small, secluded, and especially pretty campground in the Foot-hills area, with a prime location amid a grove of oaks. The only downfall is that it can get very hot in the summer because of the relatively low elevation. See p. 135.

o **Sunset Campground in Kings Canyon:** Spread over a rolling hilltop beneath tall trees, this is a peaceful place that glows late into the evening as the sun goes down. It offers some nicely secluded sites, and it's well located for hikes to some of the park's most impressive big trees. See p. 136.

The Best Primitive Campgrounds

o **Yosemite Creek Campground:** Few people venture down the 5-mile dirt road just outside Yosemite Valley on CA 120 to this great out-of-the-way spot. It lacks amenities but is far enough off the beaten path to offer solitude. If you tend to prefer roughing it, this may be your place. See p. 79.

o **South Fork Campground in Sequoia:** This is the smallest developed campsite in the park. It's just inside the park's boundary, set at 3,650 feet along the South Fork of the beautiful Kaweah River. See p. 136.

o **Atwell Mill Campground in Sequoia:** The site is situated along Atwell Creek near the East Fork of the Kaweah River in the remote Mineral King region of the park. You'll need time and patience to reach it—allow at least an hour for the curvy and narrow 25-mile road to the camp-ground—but it's well worth the trouble. See p. 136.

The Best Day Hikes

o **Vernal Fall in Yosemite:** This is Yosemite's signature hike and is a must-see for anyone with stamina. It's just 3 miles round-trip if you follow the Mist Trail, but it's all uphill and the last quarter-mile ascends 500 stairs. Once at the top, hikers are rewarded with fabulous views and enough space to lounge around like marmots in the sun before the hike back down. See p. 44.

o **Moro Rock in Sequoia:** A short but steep climb up a historic staircase that snakes through rock crevices to the top of Moro Rock. Rewards include one of the most awe-inspiring views in the Sierra Nevada. The walk offers plenty of places to rest on the way up. See p. 112.

o **Mist Falls in Kings Canyon:** This 8-mile round-trip hike climbs 1,500 feet to the spectacular Mist Falls. The hike along the way ranges from moderately strenuous to easy strolling, through woodland areas that have lots of places where you can catch your breath. See p. 117.

The Best High-Country Hikes

o **May Lake in Yosemite:** This easy, picturesque, 2.5-mile hike begins near Tioga Road, east of White Wolf (accessible by motor vehicle in summer only). Hikers find fishing but no swimming. May Lake is dead center in Yosemite National Park. It's a good place to survey the surrounding peaks, including the 10,855-foot-high Mount Hoffman rising behind the lake. See p. 50.

o **The High Sierra Trail in Sequoia:** This popular backpacking trail offers day hikers a glimpse of what's out there. It's a moderate, 10-mile hike with pretty views of the Middle Fork of the Kaweah River and the Kaweah Range. See p. 124.

o **Paradise Valley in Kings Canyon:** Hikers describe this strenuous hike as "flat-out gorgeous;" some say it's the best that can be found in King's Canyon. It extends beyond Mist Falls to a broad valley bisected by a welcoming river. The long, 14-mile round-trip hike is a bit much to do in a day, but it is possible with some planning and an early start. See p. 118.

The Best Places to Stay & Eat Inside the Parks

o **The Ahwahnee Hotel:** No surprise here—the hotel's restaurant is the best in Yosemite. But expect to pay for it—it's also the most expensive by far. See p. 65.

o **Mountain Room Restaurant at Yosemite Valley Lodge:** Some people like the Mountain Room even better than the top-rated restaurant at the Majestic. Not only is the food here top-notch, but you also can't beat the views of Yosemite Falls. See p. 84.

o **Wawona Hotel:** This classic Victorian-style lodge is outside the valley near the Mariposa Grove and is a National Historic Landmark. Built in 1879, it is a collection of six graceful, whitewashed New England-style buildings flanked by wide porches. See p. 68.

o **Wuksachi Lodge:** By far the most upscale lodging in Sequoia & Kings Canyon, this hotel near Sequoia's Lodgepole Village features a good restaurant and great views of the forest and surrounding mountains. See p. 128.

o **Silver City Mountain Resort:** Located off the beaten path in Sequoia's Mineral King area, this is an excellent choice for those seeking a woodsy experience. There are several types of cabins here, and the restaurant bakes a nice berry pie. See p. 128.

The Best Places to Stay & Eat Outside the Parks

o **Yosemite Bug (Midpines):** Born as a hostel in 1996, the Yosemite Bug is now much, much more. The place has something for everybody, with accommodations that range from tent-cabins to delightful private rooms, plus a good restaurant, a spa, and loads of personality. See p. 72.

o **Tenaya Lodge at Yosemite (Fish Camp):** This bustling, modern hotel and conference center has it all. Set on 35 acres surrounded by Sierra National Forest, Tenaya offers hotel rooms, cabins, and a full slate of organized recreational activities, including an ice rink and indoor pool. The lodge, which seems to have one foot in the Adirondack Mountains and another in the Southwest, also offers tours of Yosemite. See p. 74.

o **Evergreen Lodge (Groveland):** A rough-and-tumble Prohibition-era destination for the workers who built the dam that flooded nearby Hetch Hetchy Valley, Evergreen Lodge has been reborn as a resort in the Sierra Nevada. See p. 69.

o **Groveland Hotel (Groveland):** This renovated historic hotel, one of the grand dames of California Gold Country, was remodeled to eliminate the Victorian look in favor of a sophisticated ranch decor vibe. Standard rooms are spacious, with feather beds, antiques, down comforters, and plush robes. Suites have large spa tubs and fireplaces. See p. 69.

o **Château du Sureau & Spa (Oakhurst):** One of the standout small resorts in all of California, the lavish Château du Sureau is as close as you can get to Europe on this side of the Atlantic. The restaurant, Erna's Elderberry House, is similarly outstanding. See p. 74.

o **Savoury's (Mariposa):** Chic but casual and featuring well-oiled service, this is our favorite restaurant in Mariposa, with a menu of simple, fresh dishes that meld culinary traditions near and far. See p. 90.

o **Sequoia Village Inn (Three Rivers):** Just outside park boundaries, the Sequoia Village Inn offers charming cabin-style units. Stylishly decorated with lodgepole-pine bed frames and hardwood floors, they're great for couples and families alike. See p. 132.

o **Castillo's Mexican Food (Mariposa):** This cozy, inexpensive cantina, established in 1955, serves heaping portions of well-prepared Mexican favorites. Entrees come with salad, rice, and beans. See p. 90.

The Best Places for Reflection

o **Yosemite's Glacier Point at Night:** You're sure to be quietly overwhelmed, either by the number of stars or the way the moonlight reflects off the granite domes surrounding the valley. See p. 36.

o **Tenaya Lake in Yosemite:** The solitude and beauty of this high-altitude, crystal-clear lake (accessible by road in summer only) outshines others in the park. Tenaya Lake is larger and more dramatic, edging up against an iridescent granite landscape. See p. 54.

o **The Backcountry:** Yosemite and Sequoia & Kings Canyon offer great backcountry getaways. Modern backpacking was invented in the Sierra Nevada and remains one of the cornerstone recreational activities in the summertime here. Few places are as well suited for contemplation as a trail into the wilds. See p. 53 and p. 121.

YOSEMITE AND SEQUOIA & KINGS CANYON NATIONAL PARKS IN DEPTH

As one of America's most popular parks, Yosemite boasts some of the most spectacular views and trails in the nation. But the traffic meltdown that confronts summer visitors can cause seemingly endless delays and enormous frustration: How can you see the park if you can't find a parking place? The park service, which is charged with both conserving this special place and opening it up to the public, says it is doing its best to manage the issue, but bumper-to-bumper delays are the new normal in Yosemite during the summer. Fortunately, the crowds stick to the roads; there is always a trail less traveled. And Sequoia & Kings Canyon parks are far less crowded. Wherever you might go, this chapter will give you some background on the issues facing the parks and how to visit responsibly.

THE PARKS TODAY

Yosemite National Park, the jaw-dropping, head-turning jewel of the U.S. parks system, should be seen by everyone. Its plunging waterfalls, stark granite cliffs, alpine lakes, and grassy meadows are a vacationer's dream. And, in fact, more than 4 million people visit annually. About 95% of them, however, only explore the park's famous Yosemite Valley, a mile-wide, 7-mile-long canyon surrounded by massive domes, soaring pinnacles, and sparkling waterfalls. Some visitors leave without ever getting out of their cars, not because they want to drive through but because they are unable to find a parking place.

Overcrowding has become an all-consuming problem here, the major issue facing park officials today. Rangers say the traffic, congestion, and lack of parking are keeping them from managing the park's resources and are impacting the visitor experience.

From a traveler's standpoint, the simplest answer is to avoid the high season (May–Sept) and to go beyond the valley, where some 800 miles of marked trails offer hikers tranquility and a variety of challenges, from easy to difficult.

For park authorities, the search for answers continues. Yosemite has about 2,000 parking spaces and rangers say more will be added, but that number will still be limited.

Other changes: Parking lots have been moved, a traffic circle was built by the main store in Yosemite Village, and attempts have been made to require parking reservations. This plan didn't work in the early tests because many people made reservations and didn't show up or parked elsewhere.

One management technique that seems to be working is to give stressed areas of the park some relief during reconstruction projects.

A restoration project at the Mariposa Grove of Giant Sequoias closed the area for 3 years while a $40-million project was undertaken by the park service and Yosemite Conservancy. The 250-acre stand of trees, the largest grove of Sequoias in the park, has 500 towering trees, some of the oldest, rarest, and largest living organisms in the world. But the trees were suffering from too much congestion in the area and a lack of water.

The project's primary goals were to improve the giant sequoias' habitat and the visitor experience. Crews removed parking lots and roads, added accessible trails, and restored the natural flow of water to the sequoias. Parking was relocated 2 miles away from the grove and is now connected by shuttle buses. The restoration, the largest in the park's history, was completed in 2018.

It's a far different scenario at Sequoia & Kings Canyon National Parks. Both are crowded in summer, too, when RVs and slow drivers can form convoys dozens of cars long—but it's nothing like Yosemite.

Sequoia & Kings Canyon are far less developed, and the places that are developed are much more spread out. Frankly, officials here learned a lesson from Yosemite and worked hard not to make the same mistakes.

The parks are awe-inspiring, with rugged canyons and some of the most spectacular trees and vistas in the Sierra, but they are not crammed into a 7-mile valley, and you won't find a crowd three deep jostling for a view, as in Yosemite.

Fire is an escalating danger for all three parks, with larger, hotter, more deadly fires burning the forests of the Western U.S. as a result of climate change.

One such megafire struck Yosemite National Park in 2018, closing the park for 3 weeks as it raged through the Sierra Nevada Mountains, burning 86,000 acres of forest before jumping Highway 41 into the park and scorching another 11,000 acres within its boundaries. Three thousand firefighters battled the blaze; two died. Meanwhile, the valley choked in a cloud of smoke.

But Yosemite rangers have concluded that fire has a place in the park. After a century of fire suppression, which led to dense forests that burned quickly, fire officials now embrace periodic burns as good wilderness management. If you visit on a weekday, you may see park personnel setting small fires to remove dead wood and underbrush.

LOOKING BACK: YOSEMITE AND SEQUOIA & KINGS CANYON HISTORY

This region of the Sierra Nevada has a rich natural and cultural history. The landscape can change completely from one mile to the next. High mountain meadows give way to turbulent rivers that thunder down deep gorges, tumble over vast waterfalls, and turn into wide, shallow rivers as they meander through the next valley. Such diversity can be attributed to the region's geologic roots, which stretch back 10 million to 80 million years, when a head-on collision between two immense plates of rock formed this mountain range. The rock, weakened by extreme temperature variations, was later carved by erosion into deep valleys, including Yosemite Valley and Kings Canyon. In a process described more fully in chapter 9, the Ice Age brought glaciers that smoothed the faces of rocks such as Yosemite's El Capitan and Half Dome, some of the towering peaks of Yosemite's Tuolumne Meadows, and Kings Canyon itself.

American Indians were aware of Yosemite at least 5,000 years ago. While Egyptian scholars were making their first use of numbers, American Indians in California were living as their forebears had for thousands of years. By 1000 B.C., there were tribes—including the Ahwahneeches (Ah-*wah*-nee-ches), a subtribe of the Miwok—living in Yosemite Valley. Archaeologists have since documented 36 living sites on the valley floor that supported a vast number of inhabitants with lush vegetation and numerous animals. The largest village lay just below Yosemite Falls.

Although the early inhabitants were called Ahwahneeches, the valley was named Yosemite by soldiers sent to oust American Indians who refused to relocate to the plains. While seated around a campfire, a doctor among the group suggested the soldiers settle on a name for the valley. Among the suggestions were Paradise Valley and Yosemite, the name by which the Indian tribes in the region were known. Some were offended by the suggestion of honoring American Indians in the valley, but in the end, the name Yosemite won. Ironically, however, Yosemite was the soldiers' mispronunciation of the word Oo-*hoo*-ma-te, the name of just one settlement of Ahwahneeches, whom soldiers drove from Yosemite Valley in 1851.

The Ahwahneeches' neighbors, the Monaches (also known as the Western Monos), lived in Kings Canyon and met their end during a smallpox outbreak in 1862. The Monaches kept villages in the foothills all year long, although they sometimes moved to the forest in the summer. The Potwishas and Wuksachis were subtribes of the Monaches who also lived in the foothills around Sequoia's Ash Mountain. Kings Canyon was named in 1806 by the Spaniard Gabriel Moraga, the first European to lead an expedition in the area. Moraga's party discovered a major river on January 6, the Roman Catholic date of the Epiphany. Being a good Catholic, Moraga christened the river El Río de los Santos Reyes, or "The River of the Holy Kings," in honor of the three wise men who visited the infant Jesus on the same date. The name was later shortened to Kings River.

The land of Kings Canyon and Sequoia remained untouched until 1827, when trappers arrived. The California gold rush drew hordes more in 1849, and abandoned mines dot Sequoia & Kings Canyon National Parks, especially in Mineral King, a region unsuccessfully mined for silver in the 1800s.

Despite being plagued by natural upheavals such as prehistoric earthquakes and glaciers, Yosemite, Sequoia, and Kings Canyon survived. Then the parks faced other challenges—each was destined for destruction by dams, logging, and consequent flooding. Large stands of giant sequoia were obliterated in the late 1800s. Ranchers allowed their sheep to graze beneath the big trees. Sawmills were built, and zip-zip—down came entire forests. Adding insult to injury is the fact that the wood of the largest giant sequoias is brittle and generally pretty useless. Nevertheless, early loggers chopped down a third of the ancient trees in the region. This travesty would likely have continued if not for a few mid-19th-century conservationists who pushed the government to turn the areas into parks. In 1890, Sequoia National Park was created, along with the tiny General Grant National Park, established to protect Grant Grove. Unfortunately, the move came too late to spare Converse Basin. Once the largest stand of giant sequoias in the world, today it's a cemetery of tree stumps, the grave markers of fallen giants. One tree dates back 3,200 years.

In 1926, the park was expanded eastward to include the small Kern Canyon and Mount Whitney, but rumblings continued over the fate of Kings Canyon itself. For a while, its future lay as a reservoir. It wasn't until the 1960s that Kings Canyon was finally protected for good. In 1978, Mineral

King was added to Sequoia's half of the park, and in 2001, President Bill Clinton established Giant Sequoia National Monument in the national forest adjacent to the parks. The parks have been managed jointly since World War II.

While the fight to save the giant sequoias raged, a similar battle was taking place over Yosemite. Here the threat came from opportunists hoping to cash in on Yosemite Valley's beauty. Soon after the Ahwahneeches were driven out, homesteaders came in. They built hotels and crude homes and planted row crops and orchards.

Somehow, during the Civil War, Congress convinced President Abraham Lincoln to sign legislation protecting the valley and the nearby Mariposa Grove of giant sequoias. Yosemite Valley was, in effect, the first state and national park in America. But the thousands of acres surrounding these relatively small federal holdings were still subject to exploitation in the form of mining, logging, and grazing. Happily, on October 1, 1890, a week after approving Sequoia National Park, Congress established Yosemite National Park. The new park did not include the valley or Mariposa Grove, which were still part of the older Yosemite Valley Park, but it encompassed enormous tracts of surrounding wilderness. With two administrations—one overseeing the valley and big trees, and one overseeing the new park—the expected overlap took place and frustration mounted.

In 1906, legislators decided to add the valley and big trees to the new park and to reduce the park's size to follow the natural contours of the land, while excluding private mining and logging operations. Everyone was set to live happily ever after. No one would have predicted that Yosemite would become one of the most popular places on the planet (though some argue that tourism has accomplished the destruction that logging couldn't).

Recent years have brought more and more human activity to this wilderness haven. Today this is the biggest challenge

Impressions

Yosemite Valley, to me, is always a sunrise, a glitter of green and golden wonder in a vast edifice of stone and space.
—Photographer Ansel Adams

facing Yosemite and, to a lesser extent, Sequoia & Kings Canyon. Big changes are expected as the National Park Service grapples with the best way to permit access without causing more irreparable damage to this natural wonderland.

Who would have thought that preservation would wreak its own brand of havoc here? But we can only imagine how this beautiful place would look today had it been left in the hands of profiteers.

WHEN TO GO

YOSEMITE   Expect large crowds from May to September, especially on weekends, and on holidays. If you can only visit in summer, arrive by 8 or 9am.

A spring visit, after a winter of heavy snowfall, can be spectacular, with roaring falls putting on a robust show; visit on weekdays to avoid crowds. Winter is also a great time to explore Yosemite: Not only is the park virtually empty, but there are also many winter-only activities, from cross-country skiing, snowshoeing, and ice skating to downhill skiing and sledding at Badger Pass. Keep in mind that the high country along Tioga and Glacier Point roads is inaccessible to vehicles from mid-fall to early June, when deep snow closes the roads.

SEQUOIA & KINGS CANYON   Like Yosemite, a variety of attractions stay open at these parks all year, but Cedar Grove is closed from mid-November to mid-April, and Mineral King is closed from November 1 until Memorial Day weekend. Summertime sees a lively population of adventure seekers (see "Hikes & Outdoor Pursuits in Sequoia & Kings Canyon," chapter 7). Note that the hiking-trail passes in the high country may be snowbound until July.

CLIMATE

The climate at Yosemite, Sequoia & Kings Canyon varies considerably, depending on the region of the park. A good rule to remember is the higher you go, the cooler it gets. So pack a parka on any trip that climbs above the valley floor or ventures into the backcountry.

In summer, Fahrenheit temperatures at lower elevations (such as Yosemite Valley) can climb into the 90s (30s Celsius) and higher, and plummet into the 50s (10s Celsius) at night.

Afternoon temperatures average in the 60s and 70s (10s–20s Celsius) in spring and fall, and again, evenings are usually cool. Afternoon showers are common fall through spring. Winter days average in the 40s and 50s (5–10s Celsius), and it seldom drops below 0°F (-18°C), although much of the land above 5,500 feet is buried beneath several feet of snow.

The high country gets up to 20 feet of snow half the year, so visitors should be experienced in winter travel. November through March, it is wise to expect snow and be prepared.

Banks, government offices, post offices, and many stores, restaurants, and museums are closed on the following legal national holidays: January 1 (New Year's Day), the third Monday in January (Martin Luther King, Jr. Day), the third Monday in February (Presidents' Day), the last Monday in May (Memorial Day), July 4 (Independence Day), the first Monday in September (Labor Day), the second Monday in October (Columbus Day), November 11 (Veterans' Day/Armistice Day), the fourth Thursday in November (Thanksgiving Day), and December 25 (Christmas). The Tuesday after the first Monday in November is Election Day, which is a federal government holiday in presidential-election years (held every 4 years, and next in 2020), so expect the closures listed above.

Calendar of Events

For an exhaustive list of events beyond those listed here, check frommers.com, where you'll find a searchable, up-to-the-minute roster of what's happening in Yosemite and Sequoia & Kings Canyon.

JANUARY TO FEBRUARY

Taste of Yosemite. Yosemite hosts nationally renowned chefs who share their culinary secrets with participants. Packages that include accommodations at the Ahwahnee Hotel and the Yosemite Valley Lodge are available. Call © **888-413-8869** for reservations.

FEBRUARY

Horsetail Fall. A small waterfall that flows over the eastern edge of El Capitan in Yosemite Valley, this hidden gem becomes a star for 2 weeks in February, as the setting sun striking the water creates a deep orange glow known as the "firefall" effect. It typically starts in the middle of February and only lasts for about 2 weeks: with the correct conditions, it appears as if fire pours from the rocky monolith.

NOVEMBER TO DECEMBER

Grand Grape Celebration. California's finest winemakers hold tastings in the Yosemite Valley Lodge's Great Lounge. Each session concludes with a vintners' banquet. The five-course gala event, held in the Ahwahnee Hotel Dining Room, pairs five wines with specially selected food. Two- and three-night packages are available. Call ☏ **888-413-8869** for reservations.

DECEMBER

The Bracebridge Dinner ★★. Held on eight evenings in December, this event transports diners to 17th-century England, with music, food, and song. The festivities take place in the Ahwahnee Hotel Dining Room, bedecked with wreaths, banners, and traditional yuletide decorations. Prices change from year to year; expect to pay around $300 to $400 per person. Call ☏ **888-413-8869;** or visit www.bracebridgedinners.com for more information.

Trek to the Tree ★★★. This annual tradition, on the second Sunday in December at 2:30pm, is the main event at Kings Canyon. The Christmas ceremony takes place at the General Grant Tree, designated the Nation's Christmas Tree, and includes a solemn and moving tribute to Americans who have given their lives in service to their country. Former parks superintendent Col. John White said it best: "We are gathered here around a tree that is worthy of representing the spirit of America on Christmas Day. That spirit is best expressed in the plain things of life, the love of the family circle, the simple life of the out-of-doors. The tree is a pillar that is a testimony that things of the spirit transcend those of the flesh." The event is organized by the **Sanger District Chamber of Commerce** (www.sanger.org; ☏ **559/875-4575**).

RESPONSIBLE TRAVEL

These parks are incredibly beautiful and a joy to experience, and it is our responsibility as park visitors to keep them that way. Don't feed the animals. Don't litter. Don't take anything home that you didn't buy or bring with you. Share trails and walkways and stay on them. If this sounds like something you learned in grade school, it is, but sometimes people need a gentle reminder that 50 million years of work deserves respect.

It's relatively easy to be a good outdoor citizen—it's mostly common sense. Pack out all trash, stay on established trails, be careful not to pollute water, and do your best to have as little impact on the environment as possible. Some hikers carry a small trash bag to pick up litter. As the park service likes to remind us, protecting our national parks is everyone's responsibility.

While heavy summer auto traffic and the annual impact of millions of human beings have raised questions about the sustainability of these national parks, a visit to Yosemite and Sequoia & Kings Canyon can still be a relatively green vacation. In Yosemite, concessionaire **Aramark** (www.travel yosemite.com; ✆ **888-413-8869**) has implemented numerous environmental initiatives, including a recycling program, non-native plant–removal initiatives, and eco-friendly vehicles. Campgrounds have recycling bins near the entrances.

Perhaps the best way to think about sustainability is by connecting with the parks' wild soul via hikes on the trails and overnights in the campgrounds. One of the best ways to lessen one's impact is to go off the grid on an overnight backpacking trip. Backpacking is a refreshing counterpoint to modern life that will give perspective on the issues of sustainability and personal energy dependence. For more on backpacking, see "Special Permits & Passes," p. 171, and sections on each park's backcountry in chapters 3 and 6. Also see **Leave No Trace** (www. lnt.org) for more on the backpacker's ethic to leave any campsite in the same condition—or better—than when you found it.

TOURS

Academic Trips

The nonprofit **Yosemite Conservancy** (www.yosemite conservancy.org; ✆ **209/379-2317**) offers dozens of **Outdoor Adventures ★**, covering a range of subjects, including backpacking, natural history, and photography. Most of the programs are multi-day, with charges of about $150 per person per day (not including lodging and meals), and often include hikes or backpacking trips.

Sequoia Field Institute ★, in Three Rivers (www.sequoia history.org; ✆ **559/565-3759**), offers field seminars in and around Sequoia & Kings Canyon. The programs typically run from 1 to 4 days, with fees ranging from around $70 for the 1-day seminars to $100 per day and up for the multi-day programs. Topics vary but are likely to include subjects such as mountain wildflowers, black bears, photography, and, of course, giant sequoias. Some seminars have minimum age requirements, and some are physically demanding.

Adventure Trips

Bike-to-Hike: Ride past some of Yosemite's most famous natural landmarks on these combo biking-hiking trips organized by concessionaire Aramark at **Yosemite Mountaineering School** (www.travelyosemite.com; ✆ **209/372-8344**). You'll ride to the trailhead, then park the bike and begin your hike. Your guide will teach you about Yosemite's natural history, geology, and ecology along the way.

Southern Yosemite Mountain Guides, based in Yosemite (www.symg.com; ✆ **800/231-4575**), offers hiking, backpacking, and rock-climbing trips ideal for families and solo travelers. Options include 1-day tours of Yosemite to multiweek trips in the High Sierra. Day hikes start at $395 and overnight trips start at $525 per person.

Austin Adventures, based in Billings, Montana (www.austinadventures.com; ✆ **800/575-1540**), offers guided, family-oriented, multi-day hiking tours in Yosemite. Five-night trips run about $3,698 per person, lodging included.

Backroads, based in Berkeley, California (www.backroads.com; ✆ **800/462-2848** or 510/527-1555), offers a variety of guided walking and hiking tours, including family multi-adventure tours in the Yosemite area. Prices start at $3,499 per person, based on double occupancy, for 6 days/5 nights.

Additionally, the **Evergreen Lodge** (see p. 69) has excellent in-house recreation programs that include guided trips in and around the park. Also see "Organized Tours & Ranger Programs," p. 39, for more information.

EXPLORING YOSEMITE

High above the Yosemite Valley, a climber peers down from the sheer 3,000-foot face of El Capitan, admiring a once-in-a-lifetime view. Meanwhile, in the Valley below, a family of four stands at the base of Yosemite Falls, drenched by the mist from the waterfall's three plunges, which have a combined distance of 2,425 feet. Exploring Yosemite can be as challenging as climbing an iconic peak or as simple as walking along a short path from your car or shuttle bus. You don't have to be a mountaineer to enjoy the beauty of the park—Yosemite's most popular attractions are accessible to everyone. No matter where you go, you'll find a view worth remembering.

Active Pursuits **Hiking** is the prime recreational pursuit here, and the best views of the park's amazing waterfalls and geological formations are only accessible by foot. For starters, try the Mist Trail to Vernal Fall, the short hike to Sentinel Dome, and the trail to Cathedral Lakes in Tuolumne Meadows. Next, embark on a multiday **backpacking** trip on the John Muir Trail. The park is also one of the world's top **rock-climbing** destinations. **Skiing, rafting,** and **bicycling** are also popular.

Tours **Rangers** give talks and lead hikes in Yosemite year-round, and there are a host of guided bus tours offered by concessionaire **Aramark** and a host of other companies. If you're looking to break a sweat, **Yosemite Mountaineering School** offers guided hikes and **Southern**

Yosemite Mountain Guides takes visitors on guided hiking, backpacking, and climbing expeditions.

Facilities Yosemite has a range of options for overnight guests, from **spartan tent-cabins to high-end hotels;** most are located in Yosemite Valley. The park also has **13 campgrounds,** ranging from bare bones to downright civilized, as well as a **pizzeria,** a **cafeteria,** and a few **upscale eateries.** If you're in need of four walls and a ceiling, it's tough to top the **Ahwahnee Hotel;** although it's dated, it still offers the best accommodations in the park, and the most expensive.

ESSENTIALS
Access/Entry Points

There are four entrances to Yosemite: Big Oak Flat Entrance and Arch Rock Entrance from the west, the South Entrance from Fresno, and the Tioga Pass Entrance from the east. See the "Yosemite National Park" map, p. 2, to orient yourself. Upon arrival, make sure to get a copy of the biweekly *Yosemite Guide* for up-to-date information on ranger programs and other park events and activities.

Visitor Centers & Information

The largest visitor center in the park is the **Valley Visitor Center** in Yosemite Village (© **209/372-0200**), which provides information, offers daily ranger programs, and is conveniently located near restaurants and shopping. You can talk with park rangers about your plans for exploring the park; check out bulletin boards that display information on current road conditions and campsite availability (it also offers message boards for visitors); and view several exhibits on the park, its geologic history, and the history of the valley. This center provides information on bears and explores the impact that humans have on the park. A shop sells maps, books, videos, postcards, posters, and toys.

Nearby is the **Wilderness Center,** with high-country maps; information on necessary hiking and camping equipment; trail information; and a ranger on hand to answer questions, issue permits, and offer advice about the high country.

Information is also available at the **Wawona Visitor Center** and the **Big Oak Flat Information Station.** In the high country, stop in at the **Tuolumne Meadows Visitor Center**

(© **209/372-0263,** although it's always best to call 209/372-0200 in summer). For questions about visitor-related services, including tours and accommodations, see www.travelyosemite.com or call © **888-413-8869,** or internationally, © **602-278-8888.**

Fees

It costs $35 per vehicle (no per-person fee) per week to enter the valley; $30 for motorcycles, or $20 per person (16 and up) if arriving on bicycle or on foot. The Yosemite Pass, for $70, covers entry into the park for a year. Also see "Special Permits & Passes," p. 171.

Camping at a Yosemite campground costs $6 to $26 a night (www.recreation.gov; © **877/444-6777**). It's best to book as far in advance as possible if you are planning to camp during the summer, especially in Yosemite Valley. If you're unable to get your desired dates, it's worth checking back—cancellations do occur. Reservations are accepted up to 5 months in advance, from the 15th of each month. For example, a camper wanting a reservation for August 1 can apply no earlier than February 15. Additional campground information is available at www.nps.gov/yose/planyourvisit/camping.htm or by phone at © **209/372-0200.**

Regulations

The regulations here are similar to those at most other national parks—don't damage the resources, keep pets and bikes off the trails, observe campground quiet hours, and so on—but this is also **bear country,** so the storage of food, or anything that bears might think of as food, is also strictly regulated. In many cases, you'll need to place food and items that smell like they might be food (perfume and even toothpaste) in bear-proof canisters or lockers. Regulations are posted throughout the park, and you'll also receive information when you enter the park, but we strongly suggest that you carry as little food, cosmetics, and toiletries as possible.

ORIENTATION

Roads from the four main entrances to the park meet in Yosemite Valley, the most popular of the park's three destination points (the other two being Tuolumne Meadows and

Wawona). The valley is a mile wide and 7 miles long, set at about 4,000 feet above sea level, with the granite walls of Half Dome, El Capitan, and Glacier Point towering another 4,000 feet overhead. The picturesque Merced River, fed by several small brooks and creeks, winds lazily through the length of Yosemite Valley.

It's relatively easy to find your way around Yosemite. All road signs are clear and visible. At first, Yosemite Valley might seem to be a confusing series of roadways, but you'll soon realize that all roads lead to a one-way loop that hugs the valley's perimeter. It is easy to find yourself heading in the wrong direction, so be alert whenever you merge and just follow the signs.

We recommend visitors use the year-round shuttle-bus service in the Yosemite Valley; Tuolumne Meadows offers a similar service during the summer months only. Driving in any of these places during peak season—or even off season in the valley—is not fun, so use the shuttles as much as possible.

Yosemite Valley

Most people visit Yosemite to see its stunning valley, an incredible study in shadow and light. In spring, after the winter snow begins melting in the high country, waterfalls encircle it, plunging more than 1,000 feet. Green meadows and towering trees complete the picture. The great irony is that the original park boundaries, established in 1890, excluded the valley. It was only added later.

Yosemite Valley contains three developed areas: **Yosemite Village, Yosemite Valley Lodge,** and **Curry Village.** Except for the **Ahwahnee Hotel**—midway between Yosemite and Curry villages—all the hotels, restaurants, and shops can be found in these areas. **Curry Village** and **Yosemite Valley Lodge** offer the bulk of the park's overnight accommodations. Both have restaurants and a small grocery. The lodge has a large swimming pool, and Curry Village has an ice rink open in winter.

Yosemite Village is the largest developed region within the valley and is home to the park's largest visitor center and the headquarters for the National Park Service in Yosemite. The village also has a host of shops and services, including a grocery store, restaurants, the valley's only medical clinic, a dentist, a post office, and an ATM.

WHAT'S IN A name?

Before we explore the Valley any further, we should talk about some confusing changes that took place in Yosemite in 2016. The iconic site names people associate with Yosemite National Park—such as the **Ahwahnee Hotel** and **Camp Curry**—disappeared that year because of a legal battle.

The historic **Ahwahnee** became the **Majestic Yosemite Hotel; Camp Curry/Curry Village** became **Half Dome Village; Wawona Hotel** became **Big Trees Lodge; Badger Pass Ski Area** was renamed **Yosemite Ski & Snowboard Area;** and **Yosemite Valley Lodge** became **Yosemite Valley Lodge.**

The changes, which park advocates called appalling, took place when the park service awarded a 15-year, $2-billion contract to a new concessionaire, a subsidiary of Aramark Corp., allowing it to run the park's facilities.

The former vendor, DNC, part of Delaware North, had operated the hotels, bus service, and other facilities since 1993. DNC argued it should be compensated $51 million, largely for trademarks the company purchased for the hotels and other facilities.

The issue wound up in court, and was resolved just before this book went to press. In a victory for park advocates, the National Park Service reached a $12-million settlement with Delaware North, and retains the rights to the historical park names. Don't be surprised if you see maintenance employees still swapping out signage when you visit.

Check out the **Yosemite Pioneer Cemetery,** a peaceful graveyard in the shade of tall sequoias, with headstones dating back to the 1800s. There are about 36 marked graves, identifiable by horizontal slabs of rock, some etched with crude or faded writing.

Next door, you'll find the **Yosemite Museum** and the **Indian Cultural Exhibit.** Both attractions are free and provide a historic picture of the park, before and after it was settled and secured as a national treasure. The museum entrance is marked by a crowd-pleaser: the cross section of a 1,000-year-old sequoia with memorable dates identified on the tree's rings. The tree section was cut in 1919 from a tree that fell in the Mariposa Grove south of the valley in Wawona. Members of regional Indian tribes regularly speak or give demonstrations of traditional arts such as basket weaving.

Yosemite Valley

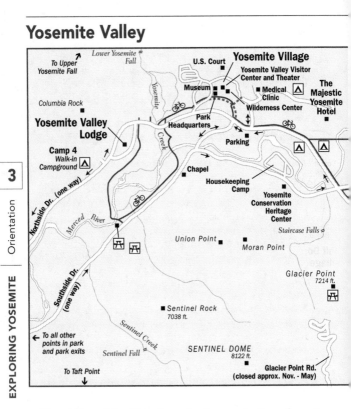

To Upper Yosemite Fall

Lower Yosemite Fall

U.S. Court

Yosemite Village

Yosemite Valley Visitor Center and Theater

Museum

Medical Clinic

The Majestic Yosemite Hotel

Columbia Rock

Yosemite Creek

Park Headquarters

Wilderness Center

Yosemite Valley Lodge

Camp 4 Walk-in Campground

Parking

Chapel

Housekeeping Camp

Northside Dr. (one way)

Merced River

Yosemite Conservation Heritage Center

Staircase Falls

Union Point

Moran Point

Southside Dr. (one way)

Glacier Point 7214 ft.

To all other points in park and park exits

Sentinel Rock 7038 ft.

Sentinel Creek

Sentinel Fall

SENTINEL DOME 8122 ft.

To Taft Point

Glacier Point Rd. (closed approx. Nov. - May)

The village of the **Ahwahneeche** (a reproduction of a real Ahwahneeche village) is behind the museum. The village offers a free self-guided walking tour that guides visitors through the transformations of the Ahwahneeche, the tribe that inhabited Yosemite Valley until the mid-1850s. The village includes a ceremonial roundhouse that's still in use.

The **Ansel Adams Gallery** (www.anseladams.com; ✆ 209/372-4413) sells prints and cards of images made by this famed photographer, in addition to pottery and other works by artisans. It also offers free photo walks and other activities.

A mile east of Yosemite Village on a narrow, dead-end road is the **Ahwahnee Hotel** (see p. 65). It's worth a visit for anyone interested in architecture and design, but the rates start north of $500 a night.

The **Yosemite Valley Chapel** is on the south side of the Merced River. From the bus stop, walk across the bridge and to

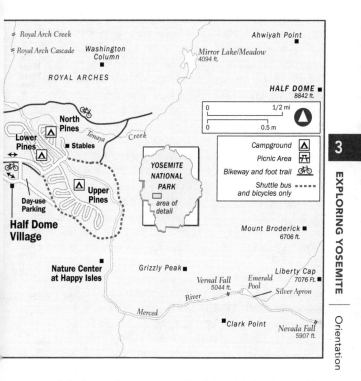

the left for just under a quarter-mile. Schedules for the worship services held in the chapel are posted in the *Yosemite Guide* newspaper and are available by phone (℗ **209/372-4831**).

The **Yosemite Conservation Heritage Center** (formerly **LeConte Memorial Lodge**) is an educational center and library run by the Sierra Club. Built in 1903 in honor of a University of California geologist named Joseph LeConte, the Tudor-style granite building hosts free educational programs and talks, which are listed in the *Yosemite Guide.*

Beyond Curry Village at the valley's far eastern end is the **Happy Isles Nature Center.** It's open April through October. The nature center offers exhibits and books about the varied animal and plant life found in Yosemite; it's a super place for children to explore.

North of the Valley

Hetch Hetchy and **Tuolumne Meadows** are remarkably different regions located on opposite sides of the park. Hetch Hetchy is on the park's western border and can be reached by taking the Evergreen Road turnoff just outside the park's Big Oak Flat Entrance. Tuolumne Meadows is on the park's eastern border, just inside Tioga Pass, and is inaccessible by motor vehicle during the winter. (Tioga Rd. is the road that leads to the meadows.)

Hetch Hetchy is home to the park's reservoir, passionately opposed by the famed conservationist John Muir and reviled by environmentalists to this day. Many believe that losing the battle over the reservoir exhausted Muir and hastened his death. Muir passed away in 1914, a year after the bill was signed to fund the dam project. Construction on the dam began in 1919 and was completed in 1923. The reservoir provides San Francisco with drinking water; the dam generates a bit of electricity for the city as well.

South of Hetch Hetchy are two large stands of giant sequoias. The Merced and Tuolumne groves offer a quiet alternative to the Mariposa Grove of Big Trees in Wawona. Both groves are accessible only on foot. The Merced Grove is a 4-mile round-trip walk that begins about 4.5 miles inside the Big Oak Flat Entrance. Although the trees here don't mirror the majesty of the Mariposa Grove, the solitude makes this a real treat for hikers. The Tuolumne Grove (about 25 trees) can be reached by a 1-mile hike (a 1- to 2-hr. round-trip).

To get into Yosemite's **high country,** go about 1½ hours east along Tioga Road, which is closed in winter between Big Oak Flat and Tioga Pass. (You'll need skis or snowshoes to access this area during the winter.) This subalpine region is low on amenities, making it the frequent haunt of those

Impressions

The big Tuolumne Meadows are flowery lawns, lying along the South Fork of the Tuolumne River . . . here the mountains seem to have been cleared away or sit back, so that wide-open views may be had in every direction.

—John Muir

Tuolumne Meadows

who enjoy roughing it, but even cushy-soft couch potatoes can enjoy the beauty up here. Glistening granite domes tower above lush green meadows, which are cut by silver swaths of streams and lakes. Many of Yosemite's longer hikes begin or pass through here. The high country is explored at length in chapter 4 (see p. 53). There are some worthwhile sights here for anyone willing to venture away from the valley masses.

Olmsted Point ★★, midway between White Wolf and Tuolumne Meadows, offers one of the most spectacular vistas anywhere in the park. Here the enormous walls of the Tenaya Canyon are exposed, and an endless view stretches all the way to Yosemite Valley. In the distance are Cloud's Rest and the rear of Half Dome. To the east, Tenaya Lake, one of the park's larger lakes (and an easily accessible one), glistens like a sapphire.

Tuolumne Meadows, about 8 miles east of Tenaya Lake, is a huge subalpine area surrounded by domes and steep granite formations that offer exhilarating climbs. The meadow is a beautiful place to hike and fish, or just to admire the scenery while escaping the crowds of Yosemite Valley. Facing the north of the meadow is Lembert Dome, at about two o'clock; and then working clockwise, Johnson Peak, at seven o'clock; Unicorn Peak, at eight o'clock; Fairview Dome, at ten o'clock; and Pothole Dome, at eleven o'clock. Up the road is the central region of Tuolumne, where you'll find a visitor center, a campground, canvas tent-cabins, and a store. Continue east to reach Tioga Lake and Tioga Pass.

South of the Valley

This densely forested region includes Wawona and the Mariposa Grove of Big Trees. A handful of granite rock formations dot the area, but they are nothing like those found elsewhere. Traveling from the valley to Wawona, you'll come across several outstanding views of Yosemite Valley. **Tunnel View,** a turnout accessed just before passing through a long tunnel along Wawona Road, provides one of the park's most recognizable vistas, memorialized on film by photographer Ansel Adams. Remember, lighting is everything in the mountains that John Muir named "The Range of Light." Tunnel View can take on dozens of different looks in a single day. You might be awed by what you see at noon but return to the popular spot 30 minutes before the setting sun disappears, and that same view can become spectacular!

Halfway between Yosemite Valley and Wawona is Glacier Point Road (closed in winter) past the turnoff to **Badger Pass Ski Area,** which winds 16 miles to spectacular **Glacier Point ★★★**. From the parking area, it's a short hike to an amazing overlook that provides a view of the glacier-carved granite rock formations all along the valley and beyond. At this point you will be at eye level with Half Dome, which looks close enough to reach out and touch. Far below, Yosemite Valley is carpeted with meadows. There are also some

Wawona

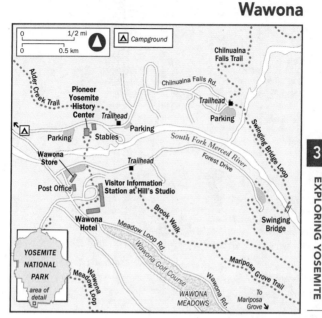

pretty sights of obscure waterfalls that are not visible from the valley floor. Glacier Point has a geology hut and a day lodge for wintertime cross-country skiers. The day lodge morphs into a gift store/snack shack during the rest of the year. Glacier Point and the lodge are accessible both on foot and by bus (see "Organized Tours & Ranger Programs," p. 39).

Continue south on Wawona Road to reach **Wawona,** a small town with a pioneer history. Located 30 miles from the valley, it was settled in 1856 by homesteader Galen Clark, who built a rustic way station for travelers en route from Mariposa to Yosemite. The property's next owners, the Washburn brothers, built much of what is today the **Wawona Hotel,** including the large white building to the right of the main hotel, which was constructed in 1876. The two-story hotel annex went up 3 years later. When Congress established Yosemite National Park in 1890 and charged the U.S. Army with managing it, Wawona was chosen as the Army's headquarters. For 16 summers, the cavalry occupied the camp and mapped the park. When Yosemite Valley was

Mariposa Grove

added to the park after the turn of the 20th century, the cavalry packed up and relocated to the valley.

Near the Wawona Hotel are Hill's Studio and the Pioneer Yosemite History Center. The studio keeps sporadic hours that are listed in the *Yosemite Guide.* This is the former workspace of noted 19th-century painter Thomas Hill; Hill painted award-winning landscapes, including some recognizable ones of Yosemite. The studio also houses the Wawona Visitor Center.

The Pioneer Center offers a self-guided walking tour of cabins and buildings that were moved to this site in 1961 from various locations in the park. Each building represents a different period in Yosemite's short history. During the summer, National Park Service interpreters dress in period clothing and act out characters from the park's past. To reach the center, walk across the covered bridge. An entertaining 10-minute stagecoach ride is offered during the summer for a small fee.

Nearby, the **Mariposa Grove** is a stand of giant sequoias, some of which date back 3,000 years. They tower almost 300 feet, are 50 feet in circumference, and weigh an average of 2 million pounds. The 500 trees here are divided into the Upper Grove and the Lower Grove. Visitors can access the Mariposa Grove via shuttle service from the new parking lot just past the south entrance off Highway 41/Wawona Road. The Grizzly Giant is the largest tree in the grove. At "just" 200 feet, it is shorter than some of its neighbors, but its trunk measures more than 30 feet in diameter at the base. A huge limb halfway up the tree measures 6 feet in diameter and is bigger than many of the "young" trees in the grove.

One of the grove's most famous trees, called the Wawona Tunnel Tree, no longer stands, but it once was very popular with visitors. In 1881, two workers carved a tunnel 10 feet high and 26 feet long through it. Thousands of visitors were photographed driving through the tree before it toppled under the weight of heavy snow during a storm in 1969. No one saw the tree fall. Another tunnel tree, the California Tree, had a tunnel cut in 1895 and still stands near the Grizzly Giant, beckoning visitors to walk through it. About ½ mile (.8 km) up from the Grizzly Giant, in a level area with more ground moisture, is the Faithful Couple. Here two large trees have fused together at their bases but remain clearly separated above.

THE HIGHLIGHTS

Spectacular **Yosemite Falls** ★★★ is a three-part waterfall that stretches 2,425 feet skyward, making it one of the tallest waterfalls in the world. In spring, snow runoff makes it a magnificent spectacle as spray crashes to the base of the falls, leaving visitors drenched. In the winter, cold temperatures help form a cone at the base of the waterfall, sometimes reaching 200 feet high—it looks like a giant upside-down snow cone. You can reach the base of Yosemite Falls by taking the shuttle bus to stop no. 6. It is also an easy walk from any parking lot near Yosemite Lodge.

Picturesque **Mirror Lake** ★, named for its nearly perfect reflection of the surrounding scenery, is slowly filling with sediment thanks to the forces of nature and, depending on the spring runoff, may be little more than a watering hole by late summer. Eventually, the sedimentation will turn the lake into a meadow. Still, the lake as it is captures beautiful images of Half Dome and North Dome, which tower above. It is surrounded by forest and has a fairly level, paved trail along its banks, which also offer places to sunbathe and picnic. It's accessible (by vehicle) to people with disabilities; there's a 60-foot elevation gain. Take the shuttle to stop no. 17.

The **Mist Trail to Vernal Fall** shows the power behind the water that flows through Yosemite. The trail itself can be slick and treacherous, but it is a pretty walk up 500 steps to the top of the waterfall (see p. 44). Miniature rainbows dot the trail as mist from the waterfall splashes below and ricochets back onto the trail. This walk is sometimes closed in winter due to ice, but there is a winter route to the top of the fall.

The remnants of a 1996 rockslide can be seen behind the **Nature Center at Happy Isles.** A granite slab collapsed with such force that it blew over hundreds of trees, claimed one life, and filled the valley with dust. Park officials decided to leave the landscape pretty much as it was post-slide, as a reminder of the tremendous geologic forces that shaped (and are still shaping) the park. In 2015 the Yosemite Conservancy provided funding to restore the existing exhibits and create new interactive panels and displays.

The **view from Glacier Point ★★★** is one of the most spectacular vistas in the park. From this point far above the valley floor, visitors will find themselves at eye level with Half Dome and hundreds of feet above most of the park's waterfalls. The white and silver rocks offer a stark contrast against the sky. To reach Glacier Point in summer, take one of the buses (check at tour desks for information) or drive south of the valley on Wawona Road to the turnoff for Glacier Point Road. Follow the winding road to the parking lot (allow about 45 min. from the valley) and walk a few hundred yards to the lookout. In winter, the road is closed and Glacier Point is accessible only on skis or snowshoes.

A **drive toward the high country** on Tioga Road offers other breathtaking views. Some of the grandest sights are at **Olmsted Point ★★**, which provides a panoramic view of the granite landscape. There are nearby picnic spots at picturesque Tenaya Lake. A bit farther along the road is the emerald-green Tuolumne Meadows, dotted with thousands of wildflowers during late spring and summer (see "Exploring the Backcountry," p. 53).

An **off-season visit** to Yosemite Valley, especially in winter, offers unique beauty plus the peace and quiet that was once commonplace. And although the high country is inaccessible by car—Tioga Pass Road and Glacier Point Road are usually closed to vehicles from mid-fall to early June, depending on snowfall—the valley becomes more accessible, because the number of visitors is greatly reduced. Snow dusts the granite peaks and valley floor, bends trees, and creates a winter wonderland for visitors. Lodging rates drop, and it is slightly easier to secure accommodations or a campground site, but even a day trip can be rewarding. Although many animals hibernate during the cold months, this is the best time of year to see the valley as it was before it became such a popular place.

SEEING THE PARK IN 1 OR 2 DAYS

This is a park that begs for an extended visit, but those with a limited amount of time will also have an enjoyable experience, especially if they make use of the park's shuttle bus. The bus is free, easy to use, and operates year-round (though with fewer stops in winter). For that reason, we've included shuttle-bus stop numbers wherever possible throughout this book. Bus stops are well marked and within easy walking distance of all parking lots.

You can get on and off the shuttles at any point, but be sure to stop in the **Valley Visitor Center** (shuttle-bus stop nos. 5 and 9) for an orientation on the forces that carved the valley. If you're not interested in taking off and exploring alone, opt for one of the guided tours (see "Organized Tours & Ranger Programs," p. 39).

The base of **Lower Yosemite Fall** (shuttle-bus stop no. 6) is an easy walk from either Yosemite Village or Yosemite Valley Lodge. From the base, you can see a portion of the magnificent water show. During peak runoff, it's not uncommon to get wet, as the force of the fall sends spray in every direction. In late winter and early spring, a huge snow cone caused by freezing water appears, rising up to 200 feet from the base of this fall. The hike up the fall is described in detail on p. 43.

Happy Isles (shuttle-bus stop no. 16) is another major attraction. Located at the convergence of several inlets, the valley's nature center is a great stop for those traveling with kids, but the area gets most of its traffic because it is also the trailhead for Vernal and Nevada falls, two picturesque staircase waterfalls that can be reached only by foot. Both hikes are described on p. 44.

We also recommend a visit to **Mirror Lake** (shuttle-bus stop no. 17), a small lake named for the near-perfect way it reflects the surrounding scenery. It's slowly filling up with silt and is less dramatic and mirror-like than it used to be, but its shore still offers a beautiful view of Half Dome. This short stroll is well marked and described on p. 44.

If you still have more time to explore, choose anything that piques your interest from a variety of hikes and activities. To make the most of your time, stick with the recommendations we list throughout the following chapters.

SEEING THE PARK BY CAR & SHUTTLE

In the eastern section of Yosemite Valley, the best way to get around is to use the park's shuttle buses. Parking is at a premium and your best bet is to find a spot, then get around by shuttle bus. The only reasons to use your private vehicle are to enter and to exit. There are also shuttles that run in Tuolumne Meadows, connecting Tuolumne Meadows Lodge with Tioga Pass and Olmsted Point (shuttles run approximately every 30 min., 7am–7pm). Elsewhere in the park,

Taking Aim at Traffic

An estimated 7,000 cars enter Yosemite National Park on any given day, leaving many visitors mired in traffic jams. To help ease the traffic volume, an in-park bus system has been in operation for more than a decade. The project, a joint effort between the National Park Service and the Yosemite Area Regional Transportation System (YARTS), shuttles visitors into Yosemite from nearby communities and commuter lots along the three highways leading into the park. For more information, visit **www.yarts.com**.

however, a vehicle is more appropriate. If you want to see the view from Glacier Point or check out Hetch Hetchy, the valley that some say was more beautiful than Yosemite's before it was flooded to become a reservoir, a car is a near necessity. However, you can always leave the driving to somebody else: Some organized tours are described below, or you can inquire at tour desks in Yosemite Village, the Ahwahnee Hotel, Yosemite Valley Lodge, or Curry Village.

Hiker's shuttles to Glacier Point and Tuolumne Meadows (www.yosemitepark.com; ℰ **209/372-4386**) are available for about $25 and $15, respectively.

ORGANIZED TOURS & RANGER PROGRAMS

The park offers many **ranger-guided walks, hikes, and other programs.** Check at one of the visitor centers or in the *Yosemite Guide* for current topics, times, and locations. Walks vary from week to week, but you can always count on nature hikes, evening discussions on park anomalies (floods, fires, or critters), and the photography program aimed at replicating some of Ansel Adams's works. (All photo walks require advance registration at the Ansel Adams Gallery in Yosemite Village.) The evening programs outside at Yosemite Conservation Heritage Center and Yosemite Valley Lodge are great for young and old alike. There are also nighttime stargazing tours at Glacier Point.

Several organizations also host guided trips. West of Yosemite, **Evergreen Lodge** (ℰ **209/379-2606;** see p. 69) offers tours of the park. Also check out **Incredible Adventures** (www.incadventures.com; ℰ **800/777-8464**), which offers 1- and 2-day day tours of Yosemite from San Francisco for about $150 to $200 per day per adult. **Southern Yosemite Mountain Guides** (www.symg.com; ℰ **800/231-4575**) offers hiking, backpacking, stock-supported, and rock-climbing trips ideal for families and solo travelers. Options range from 1-day tours of Yosemite to multi-week trips in the High Sierra. Day hikes start at $395 and overnight trips start at $525 per person. **Yosemite Mountaineering** (www.travelyosemite.com; ℰ **209/372-8344**) offers a variety of guided bikes and hikes covering 2 to 6 miles.

Discover Yosemite Tours (www.discoveryosemite.com; ☎ **559/642-4400**) conducts scheduled tours as well as customized trips. Costs run about $158 for adults, $79 for kids 3 to 15, and free for kids 2 and under. Tours are operated on small, air-conditioned buses with huge picture windows; lunch is included. The sightseeing destinations include Mariposa Grove, Yosemite Valley, and Glacier Point. Geology, flora, and fauna are pointed out along the way. Stops are scheduled for lunch, shopping, and photo opportunities. Pickup can be arranged from various hotels throughout Oakhurst and Bass Lake, as well as Mariposa and El Portal.

A variety of **guided bus tours** is also available. You can buy tickets at the tour desk at Yosemite Valley Lodge. Reservations are suggested for all tours; space can be reserved in person or by phone (www.yosemitepark.com; ☎ **209/372-4386**). Always check at tour desks for updated departure schedules and prices. Tours depart from Yosemite Valley Lodge. Adult prices range from $36.75 for a 2-hour tour to $102 for a full-day trip with lunch. Children's rates range from $27 to $64, family rates are available, and discounts are offered for seniors. The 2-hour **Valley Floor Tour** is a great way to get acclimated to the park, providing a selection of photo ops, including El Capitan, Tunnel View, and Half Dome. This ride is also available on nights when the moon is full or near full. It's an eerie but beautiful scene when moonlight illuminates the valley's granite walls and gives visitors a rare picture of Yosemite. Blankets and hot cocoa are provided. Dress warmly, though, because it can get chilly after the sun goes down. The **Glacier Point Tour** is a 4-hour scenic bus ride through the valley to Glacier Point. Tours also depart from Yosemite Valley to **Tuolumne Meadows.** The **Yosemite Grand Tour** combines Yosemite Valley, Glacier Point, and the Mariposa Grove of Giant Sequoias for a memorable day in Yosemite National Park. It last approximately 8 hours.

If you're staying in the valley, the **National Park Service** and **Aramark at Yosemite** present evening programs on the park's history and culture. Past summer programs have included discussions on early expeditions to Yosemite, the park's flora and fauna, geology, global ecology, and the legends of the American Indians who once lived here. Other programs have focused on Mark Wellman's courageous climb of El Capitan—he made the ascent as a paraplegic—and major threats to Yosemite's environment. Inquire about current programs upon check-in at your hotel or at the information booth outside the visitor center. Although most programs are held in the valley, a few campgrounds offer campfire programs in the summer. There are also nighttime walks when the moon is full.

Spring through fall, the **Yosemite Theater** offers inexpensive theatrical and musical programs designed to supplement Park Service programs. They tend to repeat from year to year, but old favorites include a conversation with noted John Muir impersonator Lee Stetson, films on Yosemite, and musical performances.

The nonprofit **Yosemite Conservancy** (www.yosemite conservancy.org; ⓒ **209/379-2317**) offers dozens of **Outdoor Adventures ★**, covering subjects such as backpacking, natural history, and photography. Most of the programs are multiday, with charges of about $125 per person per day (not including lodging and meals), and often include hikes or backpacking trips.

HIKES & OUTDOOR PURSUITS IN YOSEMITE

It's bigger than a handful of European countries and nearly the size of the state of Rhode Island, with more than 800 miles of trails. Yosemite National Park is a nature lover's paradise and a wonderful place to wander, whether you prefer paved walkways or remote trails. Park rangers lead walks and hikes, and guided day treks are also available from several organizations (see "Organized Tours & Ranger Programs," p. 39).

DAY HIKES & SCENIC WALKS

Below is a selection of day hikes throughout Yosemite National Park. Distances and times are round-trip estimates unless otherwise noted.

In & Near the Valley

Base of Bridalveil Fall ★★   Bridalveil Fall measures 620 feet from top to bottom. In the spring, expect to get wet. This walk is wheelchair accessible with strong assistance. It's a beautiful waterfall, and easy access makes it a favorite.

0.5 miles/30 min. Easy. Drive or walk to the Bridalveil Fall parking area, about 3 miles west of Yosemite Village. Follow trail markers.

Columbia Rock ★   Hike to great views on this trail, which mirrors the initial ascent of the Upper Yosemite Fall trail (see p. 46) but stops at

Columbia Rock, 1,000 feet above the valley. You won't get a valley view, but the scenery is still impressive. The trail is also less likely to get an accumulation of snow because it's on the sunny side of the valley.

2 miles/2–3 hr. Strenuous. Use the trail head for Upper Yosemite Fall (see p. 46).

Four-Mile Trail to Glacier Point ★★   This trail climbs 3,200 feet, but your efforts will be rewarded with terrific views of Yosemite Valley's north rim. Check on trail conditions before setting out; it's usually closed in winter. The trail ends at Glacier Point. If you'd like to ride up and hike down, you can catch a Glacier Point bus in the Valley (Aramark; $26 adult). To extend the hike, continue to the Panorama Trail (see p. 46), but beware: The combined round-trip distance is 14 miles.

9.6 miles/6–10 hr. Strenuous. The trail head is 1.25 miles from Yosemite Village, at the Four-Mile parking area at the marker post V-18; or take the shuttle bus to Yosemite Lodge, stop 8, and walk behind the lodge over Swinging Bridge to Southeast Dr. The trail head is 0.25 miles west.

Half Dome ★★★   Only about 300 hikers complete this dangerous and extremely strenuous hike daily, but hundreds of others hike as far as the subdome, just below the famous landmark. The Half Dome hike is the park's most famous, requiring permits and the use of climbing cables to complete. It's a long, steep trip climbing nearly 5,000 feet. From Happy Isles, take the Mist Trail past Vernal and Nevada falls into Little Yosemite Valley to the start of the Half Dome Trail. Most people turn around at the base of the subdome; those going farther need permits (www.recreation.gov or ℂ **877/ 444-6777**). The final portion of the hike, which is usually open from late May through mid-October, requires the use of cables that have been installed in the rock. Half Dome has a small level spot on top at an elevation of 8,800 feet. It's possible to break up this long trip by camping in Little Yosemite Valley. (You'll need a wilderness permit to camp.)

17 miles/10–14 hr. Very strenuous. Happy Isles, shuttle-bus stop 16.

Lower Yosemite Fall ★★   Lower Yosemite Fall is a 320-foot section of Yosemite Falls, but it packs the accumulated punch of the entire 2,425-foot waterfall, and from early spring to midsummer you're likely to get wet. You can also take this trip from Yosemite Village by following the path

HIKES & OUTDOOR PURSUITS IN YOSEMITE

Day Hikes & Scenic Walks

Hiking Trails near Yosemite Valley

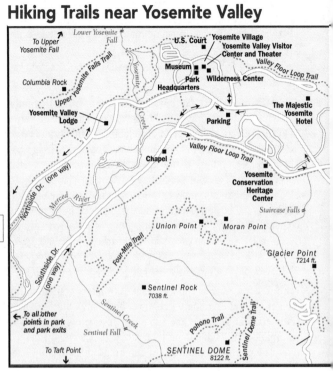

from the Valley Visitor Center to the Lower Yosemite Fall trail head. Add another half-mile, or 40 minutes, each way. This walk is wheelchair accessible with assistance.

1 mile/30 min. Easy. From shuttle-bus stop 6, follow the paved path from the Yosemite Falls parking area to the base of this waterfall.

Mirror Lake ★★   This paved trail climbs 60 feet along the west side of Tenaya Creek to the aptly named Mirror Lake, where overhanging rock formations are reflected in the lake's still surface. This trail connects with a delightful 3-mile loop around the lake, which is wheelchair accessible.

2 miles/1 hr. Easy. Shuttle-bus stop 17.

Mist Trail to Vernal Fall ★★★   This hike begins on the famous 211-mile John Muir Trail, a rugged High Sierra path that eventually ends on Mount Whitney in Sequoia & Kings Canyon National Parks. From the Happy Isles Bridge, the

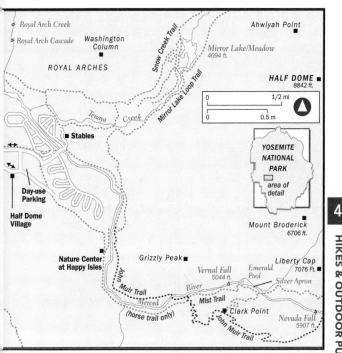

trail climbs 400 feet to the Vernal Fall Bridge, which offers water and restrooms, as well as a good view of what lies ahead. From this point, you can either take a series of switchbacks along the side of the mountain, or you can ascend the Mist Trail (our preference), which is a steep climb with 500 steps—it's wet, picturesque, and refreshing. The Mist Trail is so named because the spray from the fall drenches anyone who tackles this route, especially in spring. Be warned—it's slick and requires careful placement of your feet. Once you reach the top, you can relax on a series of smooth granite beaches and soak in the cool, refreshing water before hiking back down. You can continue up 1.2 miles to Nevada Fall and leave the crowds behind for a round-trip of 5.4 miles.

3 miles/2–3 hr. Moderate to strenuous. From Happy Isles, shuttlebus stop 16, walk to the Happy Isles Bridge. Cross the bridge and follow the signs to the trail.

Panorama Trail ★★   From Glacier Point, this trail drops 3,200 feet. At one of its prettiest points, about 1.5 miles from Glacier Point, it crosses Illilouette Falls. The path continues along the Panorama Cliff and eventually winds up at Nevada Fall, where it's a straight descent to Yosemite Valley via the Mist or John Muir trails. You can hike this trail in conjunction with Four-Mile Trail; it's also possible to take a bus to Glacier Point ($26 adult) and hike only one-way.

8.5 miles one-way/4–6 hr. one-way. Moderate to strenuous. The hike begins at Glacier Point, at the east end of the parking area.

Upper Yosemite Fall ★★★   Climb this 2,700-foot trail and you'll be rewarded with spectacular views from the ledge above the fall. Take it slowly, rest often, and absorb the scenery as you ascend higher and higher above the valley. One mile (and 1,000 ft.!) up, you'll reach Columbia Rock, which offers a good view. The rest of the trail dips and climbs, and you'll get a bit of mist from the waterfall above. The last quarter-mile is very rocky and steep, with a series of tortuous, seemingly endless switchbacks that ascend through underbrush before opening at a clearing near the top of the fall. But beware—the view here can induce vertigo. After completing the trail, it's a worthwhile walk upstream to see the creek before it takes its half-mile tumble to the valley floor below.

7.2 miles/6–8 hr. Strenuous. Shuttle bus to stop 7; the trail head is next to Camp 4 Walk-in Campground, behind Yosemite Lodge.

South of the Valley

Chilnualna Falls from Wawona ★★   One of the tallest falls outside Yosemite Valley, Chilnualna cascades down two chutes. The cascade at the bottom is narrower and packs a real punch after a wet winter. A series of switchbacks leads to the top fall. You may be splashed a bit once you reach the falls, but the trail itself is relatively dry.

8.2 miles/6 hr. Moderate to strenuous. From Wawona, take Chilnualna Rd., just north of the Merced River's South Fork, until it dead-ends at "The Redwoods," about 1.3 miles. This is the trail head.

Grizzly Giant ★   Start along the Mariposa Grove Trail at the Big Trees Loop and hike past notable trees such as the Bachelor and Three Graces, the Grizzly Giant, and

California Tunnel Tree. It's a pleasant stroll to see an impressive tree, and the hike climbs only 300 feet.

2 miles/2 hr. Easy. Trail begins at the Mariposa Grove Arrival Area.

Mariposa Grove ★★★ See famous sequoias on this wide and relatively smooth trail that follows a route people have used to access the grove for generations. Among the trees you'll pass on this somewhat strenuous route are the Bachelor and Three Graces, the Faithful Couple, and the Clothespin Tree. Continue to historic Wawona Point, an overlook with panoramic views.

7 miles/4–6 hrs. Moderate to strenuous. Begin at Mariposa Grove Arrival Area.

Sentinel Dome ★★ At the starting point, you'll be able to see Sentinel Dome on your left. The trail descends slightly; at the first fork, bear right. The way winds through manzanita and pine trees before beginning its ascent. It's a steep scramble to the top of Sentinel Dome, and you need to leave the trail on the north (left) side to clamber up. The view from the top offers a 180-degree panorama of Yosemite Valley, one of the most stunning vistas in a park that's full of them.

2.2 miles/2–3 hr. Moderate. Take Glacier Point Rd. to the Sentinel Dome parking lot, about 3 miles from Glacier Point.

Taft Point ★ The walk to Taft Point is not demanding, and it crosses a broad meadow dotted by wildflowers in early summer. On the approach to Taft Point, note the deep chasms, known as fissures, in the rock. Some of the cracks are 40 feet long, 20 feet wide at the top, and 100 feet deep. A small pipe railing farther on marks the 6×3-foot Taft Point overlook hanging over Yosemite Valley. You can test your mettle for heights here: The lookout is more than 3,000 feet up from the valley floor.

2.2 miles/2 hr. Moderate. The trail head begins at the same point as the hike to Sentinel Dome (see above). At the fork, head left.

Wawona Meadow Loop ★ This pet-friendly, relaxing stroll encircles Wawona Meadow, curving around at its east end and heading back toward the road. It then crosses the highway and winds through forest until it returns to the Wawona Hotel.

3.5 miles/1½ hr. Easy. Begin at Wawona Hotel, taking the paved road through the golf course, turning at the first left onto an unpaved fire road that loops around the meadow.

North of the Valley

Some of the day hikes discussed below can also be done as overnight backpacking trips; see "Exploring the Backcountry," p. 53.

Cathedral Lakes ★★ This is one of the busiest hikes in the Tuolumne Meadows area, but is well worth the time and effort to complete the 1,000-foot elevation gain. The lakes are set in granite bowls cut by glaciers and are surrounded by peaks and domes. Stop for a snack at the lower lake before heading up the hill to the upper lake. Parking at the trail head is limited; consider taking the shuttle bus.

7 miles/4–6 hr. Moderate. The trail head is off Tioga Rd., at the west end of Tuolumne Meadows, west of Budd Creek. Shuttle-bus stop 7.

Cloud's Rest ★★★ Hikers need to be extremely fit for this epic 2,300-foot climb that's sometimes compared to Half Dome. It begins with a descent through a wooded area, heading toward Sunrise Lakes. Ascend out of Tenaya Canyon and bear right at the junction (watch for the signposts); the vistas will appear almost at once. The sightline to your destination will be clear—a good thing, since the trail is sketchy at this point. The last stretch to the top is a little spooky, with sheer drops on each side, but your perseverance will be amply rewarded with spectacular views of the park's granite domes. Overnight stays (backcountry permit required) offer the incentive of beautiful sunrises.

14 miles/7 hr. Strenuous. Take CA 120 to Tenaya Lake. The trail begins at the parking area on the east side of the road near the southwest end of the lake.

Dog Lake ★★ Climb 600 feet through forests on this hike that offers great views of Mount Dana. Dog Lake can be chilly, but many people swim in it.

2.8 miles/1 hr. Moderate. Take CA 120 to the access road for Tuolumne Lodge. Pass the ranger station and park at the parking lot on the left. Walk north (back toward the highway) up an embankment and cross CA 120 to find Dog Lake Trail.

Elizabeth Lake ★★ This popular day hike attracts a slew of people, which can be a bummer, but it's magnificent and beautiful nonetheless—Elizabeth Lake glistens like ice. Don't forget your camera: The route is one long Kodak moment.

4.8 miles/4 hr. Moderate. Take CA 120 to the group camping area of Tuolumne Meadows Campground, where the trail begins.

Gaylor Lakes ★   This trail offers spectacular views of Tioga Rd. It begins with a 500-foot climb, then descends to an alpine lake. It's a particularly pretty hike in summer, when the mountainsides are dotted with wildflowers.

2 miles/3 hr. Moderate. Take CA 120 to Tioga Pass. The trail head is on the northwest side of the road.

Glen Aulin ★★   See a series of cascades and waterfalls along the Tuolumne River on this daylong hike. Start by heading across a flat meadow toward Soda Springs and Glen Aulin. The trail is well marked, and signs along the way do a good job of describing the area's history. Behind you, Lembert Dome rises almost 900 feet above the meadow. About a quarter mile from the trail head, the road forks; head right up the grassy slope. In less than 500 feet, you'll see a trail that leaves the road on the right and a steel sign that says GLEN AULIN IS 4.7 MILES AHEAD. This is the trail to take. Along the way, you'll pass Fairview Dome, Cathedral Peak, and Unicorn Peak. The crashing noise you'll hear in early to midsummer is Tuolumne Fall, a cascade of water that drops 12 feet, then 40 feet down a series of ledges. From here you can see a nearby High Sierra Camp. There's also a hikers' camp if you want to spend the night.

11 miles/1 long day. Strenuous. Take CA 120 toward Tuolumne Meadows, about 1 mile east of the Tuolumne Meadows Visitor Center and just a few yards east of the bridge over the Tuolumne River. Follow a marked turnoff and take the paved road on your left. The trail head begins about 0.6 miles ahead, at a road that turns right and heads up a hill toward the stables.

Lembert Dome ★   This hike offers a bird's-eye view of Tuolumne Meadows. A well-marked trail leads you to the top of the dome, 850 feet above where you began, and from there you'll see the peaks that encircle the valley, plus get good views of the beautiful meadow. It's a great place to watch sunrises and sunsets. You can combine it with the hike to Dog Lake for a 4-mile round-trip.

2.8 miles/2 hr. Moderate. The trail head is at a parking lot north of CA 120 in Tuolumne Meadows at road marker T-32. Follow the nature trail that starts here and take off at marker no. 2.

Lyell Canyon ★   Join the John Muir Trail as it follows the Lyell Fork of the Tuolumne River up an idyllic green canyon to rocky Donohue Pass, a 12-mile trek from the trail

Backcountry Hikes in Yosemite

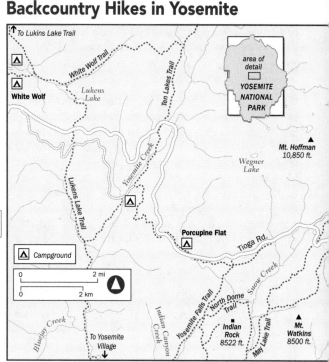

head with a 2,000-foot elevation gain. While this is a good starting point for a backcountry expedition, a shorter hike up Lyell Canyon—say, 3 miles each way—is perfect for a picnic-centered day hike. Backpackers can continue from here into the Ansel Adams Wilderness Area; day hikers can loop back through the Vogelsang area.

Up to 12 miles one-way/5 hr. one-way. Easy to strenuous. The trail head is at the Dog Lake parking lot near Tuolumne Meadows Lodge.

May Lake ★★   Winding through forests and granite, this short, picturesque hike offers ample opportunities to fish, but swimming is not allowed. Located in the center of Yosemite National Park, it is a good jumping-off point for other high-country hikes. There are numerous peaks surrounding the

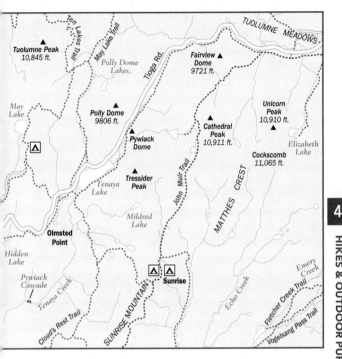

lake, including the 10,855-foot-high Mount Hoffman, which rises behind the lake. There is a High Sierra Camp here, as well as a hikers' camp on the south side of the lake.

2.4 miles/1 hr. Easy. Take CA 120 east past White Wolf; turn off at road marker T-21 and drive 2 miles to the May Lake parking area.

Mono Pass ★   You'll pass some historic cabin sites, then hike down to Walker Lake, and return via the same route. The hike loops into the Inyo National Forest and the Ansel Adams Wilderness and climbs to an elevation of 10,600 feet, 1,000 feet above where it started. There's a stupendous view of Mono Lake from the top of the trail.

8 miles/6–8 hr. Moderate to strenuous. The trail head is on the south side of CA 120 as you enter the park from Lee Vining. Drive about 1.5 miles from the park entrance to Dana Meadows, where the trail begins on an abandoned road alongside Parker Creek Pass.

Mount Dana ★ This climb is an in-your-face reminder that Mount Dana is Yosemite's second-highest peak. The mountain rises 13,053 feet and the trail gains a whopping 3,100 feet in 3 miles. The views at the top are wonderful, and once you catch your breath, you can stand upright again and stare at them in awe. You can see Mono Lake from the summit. In summer, wildflowers add to this hike's beauty.

7 miles/5 hr. Very strenuous. The trail head is on the southeast side of CA 120 at Tioga Pass.

North Dome ★★ You haven't really seen Half Dome until you've stood across the Valley on the top of North Dome and looked at it. Walk south down the abandoned road toward the Porcupine Creek Campground. A mile past the campground, the trail hits a junction with the Tenaya Creek and Tuolumne Meadows Trail. Pass a junction toward Yosemite Falls and head uphill toward North Dome. The ascent is treacherous because of loose gravel, but from the top you can catch an all-encompassing view of Yosemite Valley, second only to the view from Half Dome.

8.8 miles/5 hr. Moderate. Take CA 120 east to Porcupine Flat Campground, past White Wolf. About 1 mile past the campground is a sign for Porcupine Creek at a closed road. Park in the designated area.

Polly Dome Lakes ★★ This hike is easily the road least traveled. The trip to Polly Dome Lake is a breeze, and you'll find nary another traveler in sight. There are several lakes beneath Polly Dome that can accommodate camping. The trail fades in and out, so watch for markers. It crosses a rocky area en route, then skirts southeast at a pond located just after the rocky section. Polly Dome Lake is at the base of—you guessed it—Polly Dome, a visual aid to help hikers stay the course.

13 miles/6 hr. Easy to moderate. Take CA 120 past White Wolf to Tenaya Lake. Drive about 0.5 miles to a picnic area midway along the lake. The trail head is across the road from the picnic area.

Soda Springs ★ Take a short break on this easy trail that crosses Tuolumne Meadows and then crosses Tuolumne River on a wooden bridge. It's peaceful and beautiful, with the sound of the river gurgling along as it winds slowly through the wide expanse of Tuolumne Meadows.

1.5 miles/1 hr. Easy. Two trail heads: The 1st is at a crosswalk just east of the Tuolumne Meadows Visitor Center. The 2nd leaves from a parking lot north of CA 120 at road marker T-32. Follow the gravel road around a locked gate.

Sunrise Lakes ★ Hike to a trio of small lakes on this trail through quiet wooded glades. Look for a sign that says SUNRISE; then follow the level road to Tenaya Creek, cross the creek, and follow the trail to the right. The hike parallels Tenaya Creek for about 0.3 miles, then moves away through a wooded area and climbs gently up a rocky rise. After a while, the trail descends quickly to the outlet of Mildred Lake. Here you'll be able to see Mount Hoffmann, Tuolumne Peak, and Tenaya Canyon. At the halfway mark, the trail passes through a hemlock grove and comes to a junction. Head left (the trail on the right goes toward Cloud's Rest). About 0.3 miles from the junction, you'll reach Lower Sunrise Lake, tucked into the slope of Sunrise Mountain. The trail climbs past Middle Sunrise Lake and continues upward along a cascading creek coming from Upper Sunrise Lake. The trail follows the lake's shore and opens in less than 0.5 miles onto a wide, bare, sandy pass. Before you is the snowcapped Clark Range. The trail begins its descent, sharply switching back and forth in some places. There is a High Sierra Camp and backpackers' camp a short distance above Upper Sunrise Lake.

6.6 miles/5–8 hr. Moderate to strenuous. Take CA 120 to Tenaya Lake. The trail begins in the parking area on the east side of the road near the southwest end of the lake.

Near Hetch Hetchy

Carlon Falls ★★ This trail off the road to Hetch Hetchy takes visitors through a nicely treed river canyon to a year-round waterfall and a picturesque swimming hole.

4.5 miles/2 hr. Easy. From the turnoff to Hetch Hetchy, park immediately after the first bridge and take the trail running west of the river.

5 miles/2 hr. Moderate. The trail begins at O'Shaughnessy Dam at the end of Hetch Hetchy Rd.

EXPLORING THE BACKCOUNTRY

Backcountry hiking and sleeping beneath the stars are some of the finest adventures available in Yosemite, but 95% of the more than four million people who visit each year never leave the valley. A wild, lonelier Yosemite awaits the hardy 5% who seek the trail less traveled. Most hikers, especially serious backpackers, head into the high country. Tioga Pass via CA 120 is the gateway; once through the pass, the Sierra presents meadows of wildflowers, stark granite domes, and shimmering rivers and lakes.

Most backpackers set out on their own, as we discuss below, but guided backpacking trips (including overnight trips) are also available with **Yosemite Mountaineering** (www.yosemitemountaineering.com; ⓒ **209/372-8344**), **Southern Yosemite Mountain Guides** (www.symg.com; ⓒ **800/231-4575**), and **Backroads** (www.backroads.com; ⓒ **800/462-2848**). Rates typically start at about $150 to $200 per person per day and go up for smaller parties or expeditions that include Half Dome. Techniques and skills are taught along the way. Meals are included on longer trips. Private excursions are available, as is transportation to and from the trail heads. Gear is available for rent.

A car is much more important in Yosemite's high country than in the valley. If you don't bring your own vehicle, there is a once-a-day shuttle bus from the valley to Tuolumne Meadows. The bus leaves the valley at 8am and will let you off anywhere along the route. The driver waits in Tuolumne Meadows for 2 hours before heading back to the valley, where the bus arrives at about 4pm. The fare is about $15 one-way, slightly less for those who hop off midway. In addition, the park offers a free summer-only shuttle bus from Olmsted Point to Tioga Pass, with stops at the lodge, campground, and visitor center.

Tuolumne Meadows is a wide, grassy expanse bordered by the Tuolumne River and tall mountains. Several peaks rise high overhead and offer challenging hiking and rock climbing. In spring and midsummer, the meadow fills with wildflowers and turns an emerald green. Fishing in the river is popular, and several hikes begin in the meadows. Facilities include a general store that stocks last-minute hiking supplies, a slew of canvas tent-cabins (often all full in summer), and a restaurant.

In addition to Tuolumne Meadows, **Tenaya Lake,** set in a bowl of granite surrounded by sheer slopes, is a beautiful destination en route to the high country. Tenaya Lake offers canoeing, hiking, fishing, and sailing. It's also open to swimming for those who don't mind dunking in the chilly water— it generally remains frigid until late summer. There's ample parking and a picnic area, and many hikes lead from here to the high country.

White Wolf is midway between the valley and Tuolumne Meadows (west of Tenaya Lake). It offers a campground, canvas tent-cabins, a small store, and a restaurant. The scenery here is less dramatic, but it serves as a starting point for many hikers going into the Hetch Hetchy area. In the winter, this region is accessible only on snowshoes or cross-country skis.

Like any backcountry experience, staying in the high country—or anyplace outside the valley—requires advance planning and, if you're a beginner, a reasonable itinerary. Planning a 5-day excursion your first time out wouldn't be wise. But an overnighter, or 2 nights out, is reasonable, and Yosemite has hikes that can accommodate and reward those who venture—even briefly—off the well-paved path.

In addition, the park has five **High Sierra Camps** that provide food and shelter, allowing hikers to shun heavy backpacking gear with the knowledge that someone a few miles ahead has everything under control. All camps fill quickly via a lottery system, and reservations are necessary.

The camps—May Lake, Glen Aulin, Vogelsang, Sunrise, and Merced Lake—are situated about a day's walk apart, and each is a sort of rustic resort. Tent-cabins are furnished with woodstoves, folding tables and chairs, and beds with blankets or comforters; guests must bring sheets and towels. Soap and candles are also provided.

Most tents sleep four, but some accommodate only two people. This means you'll often be sharing your tent with strangers, but the camps tend to attract people who rank high on the camaraderie scale, so that's not usually a problem. Breakfast and dinner are served family style in a dining tent. The food is excellent and portions are generous. One dinner meal included pasta, filet mignon, soup and salad, eggplant Parmesan, and cookies. Breakfast is substantial as well. Box lunches are available for an additional charge. All you need to bring is day-hike gear (including plenty of water or a purifier), plus a flashlight, personal toiletries, something to sleep in, a change of clothes, and bed linen. In spring, trekking poles are also handy for crossing streams.

Camps are open from mid-June to around Labor Day, conditions permitting. Each camp accommodates 30 to 60 guests; demand exceeds supply, so accommodations are assigned by lottery. Applications are accepted from November 1 to November 30. The lottery drawing is held in mid-December, and guests are notified by the end of February. Cancellations are frequent, however, so it's worth a last-minute call to see if space is available. Overnights at the camps cost $151 per adult and $91 per child for lodging and meals (breakfast and dinner; sack lunches are available for an extra fee); there are also packages for multiday saddle trips and guided hikes. A meals-only option is available (about $46 per adult, reservations required) if you want to bring your own tent and eat at the camp. Sack lunches run about $15. For information or to request an application for High Sierra Camp accommodations, visit www.travelyosemite.com or call © **888/413-8869.**

4 Preparing for Backcountry Trips

Be sure to get a detailed topographical map before setting out on any overnight hike. Maps are available at many stores, visitor centers, and ranger stations throughout Yosemite National Park.

PERMITS & FEES   All overnight backpacking stays require a wilderness permit, available by phone, by mail, or in the park. Permits can be reserved 24 weeks before the permit office is open (Nov or Oct) and cost $5, plus $5 for each person on the permit. Reservations are accepted, usually beginning in late winter. Call © **209/372-0740** or visit www.nps.gov/yose/planyourvisit/wpres.htm. There you'll find the new online reservation form along with instructions for its use.

If advance planning isn't your style, first-come, first-served permits are available up to 24 hours before your trip. Permit stations are located at the Yosemite Valley Wilderness Center, Wawona Information Station, Big Oak Flat Information Station, Hetch Hetchy Entrance Station, and Tuolumne Meadows Wilderness Center. (Many of these are open in summer only; Badger Pass is the lone winter-only permit station.) Permits for the popular trails, such as those leading to Half Dome, Little Yosemite Valley, and Cloud's Rest, go quickly. Call © **209/372-0200** for permit station locations and hours.

To get a permit, you must provide a name, address, telephone number, the number of people in your party, the method of travel (snowshoe, horse, foot), the number of horses or other pack animals if applicable, start and end dates, start and end trail heads, and principal destination. Include alternative dates and trail heads as well. **Do not neglect getting a permit.** You can expect to encounter a ranger at some point along your route. You may hike for a week and never run into a ranger, but one is guaranteed to show up and ask to see your permit just as you are re-entering civilization.

SPECIAL REGULATIONS & WARNINGS Campfires are not allowed above 9,600 feet, and everything you take in must be packed out. Bears live in the high country, so stay alert: Backpackers are required to take bear-proof canisters for storing food. They can be rented for $5 a trip (and a $95 deposit on a credit card) at the Yosemite Valley Wilderness Center and several other park locations.

In the summer months, mosquitoes are public enemy number one, so bring plenty of repellent. Pack sunscreen, since much of Yosemite's high country is on granite, above the tree line. Stay off high peaks during thunderstorms, and don't attempt a climb if it looks as though a storm is rolling in: The peaks are magnets for lightning.

Overnight Hikes

Note that trail heads along Tioga Road are accessible only on snowshoes or cross-country skis in winter, as the road is usually closed due to snow from November until June.

Chilnualna Falls/Buena Vista Peak Loop ★ Although rather difficult, this trek is satisfying, as it takes you from a stunning waterfall through meadows and forests to some lovely lakes. The first day's hike is 8 miles, to Chilnualna Falls, one of the park's tallest falls outside the valley. It's a strenuous climb up. The bottom fall tumbles down a narrow chute, and 50 feet up is yet another fall; the combination is a vision in spring with a strong winter runoff. Above the falls, the trail ascends via switchbacks up a gorge to a junction. One route will lead through forests toward Bridalveil Campground, the other toward Chilnualna Lakes. Take the Chilnualna Lakes route. Just below this junction are several nice places to camp overnight. There are also swimming holes nearby.

From here, you'll climb along the headwaters of the creek to a set of high-altitude lakes. About 2.5 miles up is Grouse Lake Creek. This can be a tough cross during high water, and the rock is very slick, so be careful. Head north (left) for about

0.5 miles after the crossing toward Turner Meadows. At the next junction, head right (east) toward Chilnualna Lakes, about 5 miles away. Buena Vista Peak rises above the lakes. Campsites are plentiful in this area. From the lakes, head up into 9,040-foot Buena Vista Pass. At the pass, hike south on Buena Vista Trail toward Royal Arch Lake. The next junction goes right (west) toward Johnson, Crescent, and Grouse lakes. After Grouse Lake is the Grouse Lake Creek crossing and the return trail to Chilnualna Falls and the parking area.

28.5 miles/4 days. Moderate to strenuous. Take CA 41 to Wawona in Yosemite National Park. Turn east on Chilnualna Rd. and stay on this road for about 1⅓ miles until you reach "The Redwoods," where the road ends. This is the trail head.

Ten Lakes Trail ★   The trail is well marked and picturesque, with lots of rocks to climb around on and several lakes for swimming. The trail offers some great fishing for brook and rainbow trout. Mosquitoes can be a major deterrent here in summer, however. Backpackers camp at the designated campground at May Lake or in an undeveloped spot at least a quarter-mile from the shore. There are numerous places to camp, so it's best to discuss options with a ranger.

12.6 miles/2 days. Moderate. On CA 120 east, pass the White Wolf Campground to the trail-head parking lot, just before a bridge and Yosemite Creek sign. The trail head is on the north side of the road.

Tuolumne Meadows to Agnew Meadows along the John Muir Trail ★★   This high-altitude climb offers visitors a weekend getaway that leaves flatlanders breathless and displays some of the eastern Sierra's most pristine beauty. Be warned—it's a real heart-thumper. You'll trek through Donohue Pass at 11,056 feet. From the pass, it's mostly downhill. Campers should discuss the numerous overnight options with a park ranger before heading out. You can return the way you came—perhaps exploring the Vogelsang area on your way out—or follow the John Muir Trail to Red's Meadow near Mammoth and Devil's Postpile, or loop back into Yosemite over the truly strenuous switchbacks over 12,260-foot Koip Peak Pass.

28 miles/3 days. Strenuous. The trail head begins where the above hike (Ten Lakes Trail) ends, or take CA 120 to Tuolumne Meadows and the Dog Lake trail head parking area for the John Muir/Pacific Crest Trail/Lyell Fork hikes.

| Impressions |

> *Thousands of tired, nerve-shaken, overcivilized people are*
> *beginning to find out that going to the mountains is going*
> *home; that wilderness is a necessity.*
>
> —John Muir

Yosemite Creek ★★ You can avoid the steep climb
from the valley floor on this hike that approaches Yosemite
Falls from behind and ends up at the same place as the Upper
Yosemite Fall hike (see p. 46). After hiking 2 miles, you'll
see the Yosemite Creek Campground; walk through the
campground to the Yosemite Falls Trail. In about 0.8 miles,
you'll hit another junction. Head left (south) and hike for
another 4 miles to Upper Yosemite Fall. The view from here
is heart-stopping. The valley looks Lilliputian with its tiny
lodges, people, and cars far below. The waterfall is surrounded by slick rock, so be careful, especially in wet conditions; it seems that every year someone slips over the edge
into the abyss below. You can hike back the way you came,
or head down the path to the valley if you've got a shuttle
system set up or someone to take you back to your car. As
with all overnight hikes, discuss camping options with a
ranger before heading out.

17 miles/2 days. Moderate to strenuous. Take CA 120 east past the
White Wolf Campground to the trail head, which is just before a
bridge sign for Yosemite Creek. The trail head is on the south side
of the highway.

**Yosemite Valley to Tuolumne Meadows along the
John Muir Trail** ★★ This popular wilderness hike is a
challenging trek along the John Muir Trail that covers 20 to
25 miles, depending on detours, and features an elevation
gain of more than 4,000 feet. The trail is well marked and
heads from the valley floor past some of the best waterfalls
you'll see on your journey, Vernal and Nevada falls. You'll
also pass Half Dome and then up to Cathedral Peak. Cathedral Lakes are nearby and worth a side trip. Camp at
Tuolumne Meadows.

22 miles/2 days. Moderate to strenuous. The trail begins in the valley at the Happy Isles parking area.

Side Trips from High Sierra Camps

Glen Aulin High Sierra Camp to Waterwheel Falls ★

This walk is long and arduous but takes you to six major waterfalls along the Tuolumne River. You'll climb about 1,000 feet along open ledges on the river. There's a lot to see, so get an early start. The trail switches along the noisy Tuolumne, plunges into a forest, and meanders across a meadow. The most notable waterfalls begin about 1.5 miles into the hike and range from long ribbons to 50-foot-long, 20-foot-wide masses of white water. The trail descends through a canyon. Watch for signs to Glen Aulin (about 3.5 miles away). You'll see LeConte Fall on your left beyond a few campsites. It cascades in broad, thin sheets of water, some stretching 30 feet wide as they flow down steeply sloping ledges along the river. A half-mile past LeConte is the top of Waterwheel Falls, a set of long, narrow falls that roar through a trough in the ledge to the left of the trail. With enough water and force, some of the water hits the ledge rock with sufficient force to propel it upward and back in a circle, like a pinwheel. Backward water wheels are rare and should not be confused with the upward-and forward-spinning water wheel of LeConte Fall. You can climb down to and back from Waterwheel Falls—it'll add a steep 0.3 miles to your trip—before returning to Glen Aulin.

7.6 miles/8 hr. Strenuous (but worth it). Cross Conness Creek; the trail head is on your left about 30 ft. ahead.

Sunrise High Sierra Camp to Upper Cathedral Lake ★

Views of the stunning Cathedral Peak are the highlight of this hike. Descend the stone steps to the John Muir Trail along the north side of a meadow. The trail skirts the meadow and crosses several small creeks. Stick to the John Muir Trail, which will bring you to a branch of Cathedral Fork, which has a riverbed lined with rust-colored rocks. After 2 miles, the trail falls away from the creek and toward Columbia Finger, climbing a rocky slope that quickly levels off. You'll see a variety of peaks along the way, and toward the end, when Cathedral Peak comes into view, you'll be surrounded by 2-mile-high pinnacles that somehow escaped the prehistoric glaciers. The trail descends through a meadow, then on to Upper Cathedral Lake. The trek back to camp offers stunning views from the reverse perspective.

10 miles/6–8 hr. Moderate to strenuous. The hike begins next to the dining tent.

Vogelsang High Siera Camp to Vogelsang Pass ★

This hike offers broad views of an assortment of peaks. Turn left from the trail where it crosses the creek (just past the intersection of the pass trail and the camp trail), walk 50 feet upstream, and cross the creek. You'll find nothing but spectacular views. The two towers of Vogelsang Peak lie before you, stretched apart like some enormous saddle, along with views of Vogelsang Lake. The rough slopes of Vogelsang Pass are straight ahead; a 50-foot-wide pond surrounded by pinkish granite marks the top of the pass. Cross to the north side for one of the most spectacular views in the High Sierra. Walk a few feet more, to the point where the trail begins to descend toward Lewis Creek, and a magnificent panorama will greet you: 12,080-foot Parson's Peak; 12,503-foot Simmons Peak; 12,960-foot Mount Maclure; the wide 12,561-foot Mount Florence; the summits of Clark Range, Triple Divide, and Merced peaks; the aptly named Red and Gray peaks; and Mount Clark. Look down and you'll see the blue-green Bernice Lake.

3 miles/2–3 hr. Moderate to strenuous. The walk begins on the west side of the dining tent and descends to Fletcher Creek.

OTHER SPORTS & ACTIVITIES

About the only thing you can't do in Yosemite is surf. In addition to sightseeing, Yosemite is a great place to bike, ski, rock-climb, fish, and even golf.

BICYCLING   There are 12 miles of designated bike trails in the eastern end of Yosemite Valley, which is the best place to ride, since roads and shuttle-bus routes are usually too crowded and dangerous for bicyclists. Children 17 and under are required by law to wear helmets. During the summer, single-speed bikes (and kiddie trailers) can be rented by the hour ($12; $20.25 with trailer) or the day ($34; $61 with trailer) at **Curry Village** (© **209/372-8323**), and at **Yosemite Valley Lodge** (© **209/372-1208**). Bike rentals include helmets for all ages. See www.travelyosemite.com/things-to-do/biking for details.

CROSS-COUNTRY SKIING   The park has more than 350 miles of skiable trails and roads, including 25 miles of machine-groomed track and 90 miles of marked trails in the Badger Pass area. Equipment rentals, lessons (including excellent beginner lessons), and day and overnight ski tours to the Glacier Point Ski Hut ($143 to $550 per person per trip, depending on the number of people and days, and whether the trip is guided) are available from Yosemite Cross-Country Center and Ski School (www.travelyosemite. com; © **209/372-8444**).

FISHING   Several species of trout are found in Yosemite's streams. Information is available from the **California State Department of Fish and Wildlife** (www.wildlife.ca.gov; © **916/928-5805**). There are also special fishing regulations in Yosemite Valley; get information at the visitor centers.

GOLF   There's one golf course in the park plus several others nearby. **Wawona Golf Course** (© **209/375-6572**) sports a 9-hole, par-35 course that alternates between meadows and fairways. Greens fees are $24 for 9 holes, cart not included.

HORSEBACK RIDING   Several companies offer guided horseback rides in and just outside the national park, with rates starting at $67 for 2 hours and $140 for a full day. **Yosemite Stables** (© **209/372-8348**) offers rides from Yosemite Valley, Tuolumne Meadows, and Wawona; it leads multiday pack trips into the backcountry (call for details). **Wawona Stable** (www.travelyosemite.com; © **209/375-6502**) offers rides just south of Wawona.

ICE SKATING   The outdoor ice rink at **Curry Village,** with great views of Half Dome and Glacier Point, is open from early November to March, weather permitting. Admission is $9.75 for adults, $9.25 for children; skate rental costs $3.75, helmets are free. Call © **209/372-8333** for current hours.

RAFTING   A raft-rental shop is located at **Curry Village** (© **209/372-8319**). Daily fees are $28.50 per person. Children under 50 lbs. are not permitted in rental rafts. Includes a raft, paddles, mandatory life preservers, and transportation from Sentinel Beach to Curry Village. Be aware that swift currents and cold water can be deadly. Talk with rangers and shop employees before venturing out to be sure the trip you're planning is within your capabilities.

ROCK CLIMBING   Yosemite is considered one of the world's premier playgrounds for both experienced rock

Many of the organizations listed in this section offer special programs for children, including rock climbing and ski lessons. In addition, Yosemite has **Little Cub** and **Junior Ranger** programs, plus special walks and activities for kids. See "Family Travel," in the "Fast Facts" section on p. 175.

climbers and wannabes. The **Yosemite Mountaineering School** (www.yosemitemountaineering.com; ✆ **209/372-8344**) provides instruction for beginning, intermediate, and advanced climbers in the valley and Tuolumne Meadows April through October. Classes last from a day to a week; private lessons are available as well. Rates, which include all equipment, vary according to the class or program; lessons are about $172 to $215 a day, and guided climbs are around $379 per day for one person or $252 or less per person for two.

SKIING **Badger Pass Ski Area** (www.travelyosemite.com; ✆ **209/372-1000**) is usually open from mid-December to early April, weather permitting. This small resort, located 22 miles from Yosemite Valley, was established in 1935, making it the oldest downhill operation in California. There are 10 runs, rated 35% beginner, 50% intermediate, and 15% advanced, plus a park and tubing area, with a vertical drop of 800 feet from the highest point of 8,000 feet. There are five lifts—one triple chair, three double chairs, and a cable tow. Full-day lift tickets cost $47 for adults, $29.50 to $42 for kids 7 to 17 (kids under 7 are free); half-day tickets are $40, and $22 to $35, respectively. Seniors 65 and over ski free Monday through Thursday. There are ski shuttles from Yosemite Valley and Oakhurst, as well as some great ski-and-stay packages.

Facilities at the ski area include several casual restaurants; a ski shop; ski repairs; a day lodge; lockers; and an excellent ski school, thanks to the late "Ski Ambassador" Nic Fiore, a Yosemite ski legend who arrived in the park in 1947 to ski for a season and never left. Fiore became director of the ski school in 1956, and park officials credit him with making Badger Pass famous and creating a family-oriented ski area where generations have learned the art of skiing.

4

HIKES & OUTDOOR PURSUITS IN YOSEMITE

Other Sports & Activities

WHERE TO STAY & EAT IN YOSEMITE

Serenity settles over Yosemite National Park after dark. The day-trippers are gone and sounds of the forest supplant the noise of vehicles and exuberant sightseers. Spending a night in the park, whether camping or staying in a lodge, is a trip highlight. Yosemite Valley, the hub for lodging, dining, and other services, is crowded in summer, but it offers the best location—close to Yosemite's main attractions and with easy access to the park's shuttle-bus system.

5

Choices are also available outside the valley but still within the park: You can camp at Wawona, Tuolumne Meadows, White Wolf, and a host of other sites; there are lodges and privately owned cabins as well.

In addition, visitors can find excellent accommodations, campgrounds, and restaurants outside the park in the gateway communities of El Portal, Mariposa, Oakhurst, Lee Vining, and Groveland.

LODGING
Inside the Park

Many historic names within the park disappeared in 2016 because of a legal battle between the National Park Service and Yosemite's former concessionaire, Delaware North. A settlement was reached in mid-2019, and Yosemite's beloved lodgings are once again known by their historic names: Ahwahnee Hotel, Curry Village, and Wawona Hotel. Only Yosemite Valley Lodge chose to retain its new name.

Lodging within the park is now run by Aramark, a major player in the hospitality industry, with management duties at more than 60 destinations across the U.S. Rooms can be reserved up to 366 days in advance by calling (℗ **888/413-8869,** visiting **www.travelyosemite.com** or writing to Aramark, Q850, E. Camelback Rd., Suite 240, Phoenix, AZ 85016. Summer fills up fast; make reservations as far in advance as possible.

Also, more than 120 private homes in the park can be rented through **Redwoods in Yosemite,** 8038 Chilnualna Falls Rd., CA 95389 (www.redwoodsinyosemite.com; (℗ **877/753-8566**). Accommodations range from small cabins to large vacation homes, all furnished and equipped with linens, cookware, and dishes. Summer rates range from $260 a night for a one-bedroom cabin to $750 or more for a five-bedroom rental; there are usually 2- or 3-night minimum stays. It's perfect for families traveling with a pet; none of the other lodges in the park allow animals.

Cabins can also be rented from Yosemite West Lodging (www.yosemitewestreservations.com; (℗ **559/642-2211**), which has about 25 cabins inside the park and another 25 outside it. Rates range from $136 to $500 a night depending on the season.

EXPENSIVE

Ahwahnee Hotel ★★★   Although it's a bit dated, this hotel is fit for a king or queen—and it has hosted both. Queen Elizabeth II slept here, as did U.S. President John F. Kennedy. It's tough to top the stately Ahwahnee, a six-story concrete-and-stone structure that offers beautiful views from nearly every window. The Great Lounge features three fireplaces large enough to stand in, plus overstuffed sofas and chairs that are the perfect spot for reading or playing games after a day of hiking. Regular guest rooms, renovated in 2017 and 2018, offer a choice of two doubles or one king-size bed (often with a couch).

Yosemite Valley, Yosemite National Park. www.travelyosemite.com. (℗ **888/413-8869.** 121 units. $417–$519 double; $536–$1,146 suite. Parking available or take the shuttle bus to stop no. 3. **Amenities:** Restaurant (see p. 83); bar; concierge; outdoor pool; room service; afternoon tea; gift and sweet shops on site; free Wi-Fi.

Yosemite Valley Lodge ★★   An eco-friendly facelift, complete with recycled carpeting, and energy-saving lights and TVs, has updated this popular lodge located near Yosemite Falls. Most units feature balconies or patios, some with spectacular views of Upper Yosemite Fall. The lodge is comfortable and clean, but more practical than fancy. It's not uncommon to see deer and other wildlife scampering through this area. Spring mornings bring a wonderful orchestra of songbirds and stunning views at sunrise.

Yosemite Valley, Yosemite National Park. www.travelyosemite.com. ℂ **801/559-5000.** 245 units. $258 double. Additional $10 per extra adult. Lower rates Nov–Mar. Parking available or take the shuttle bus to stop no. 8. **Amenities:** 2 restaurants (see "Where to Eat," p. 83); lounge; bikes; children's programs; large outdoor pool; free Wi-Fi.

MODERATE

Curry Village ★   Some people have a love-hate relationship with Curry Village. On the plus side, it is in a prime location in Yosemite Valley. However, it features more than 400 canvas tents that are packed tightly together. There are too many people and too much noise, especially on a hot summer day when temperatures sometimes top 100 degrees. The camp was founded in 1899 as a cheap lodging option for valley visitors at a mere $2 a day, but guests can kiss those $2 days goodbye. Still, it's an economical place to crash, and it gives you the feel of a camping vacation without the hassle of bringing your own tent. Note that since these tents are basically canvas affairs, and this is bear country, you'll need to lock up all foodstuffs—and anything that bears might think is food, like toothpaste—in bear-proof lockers, which may be a healthy walk from your tent-cabin.

The canvas tents have wood floors, sleep two to four people, and are equipped with beds, bedding, dressers, and electrical outlets; some have propane heaters. Much more substantial and comfortable are Curry Village's 50 or so attractive wood cabins with private bathrooms. There are also 14 more spartan wood cabins that, like the tent-cabins, share a large bathhouse, and 18 motel rooms.

Yosemite Valley, Yosemite National Park. www.travelyosemite.com. ℂ **801/559-5000.** 500 units. $114–$149 double tent-cabin; $121–$175 double cabin without bathroom; $170–$240 double cabin with bathroom; $273 double motel room. Lower winter rates. Parking available, or take the shuttle bus to stop no. 13, 14, or 20. **Amenities:**

Lodging

WHERE TO STAY & EAT IN YOSEMITE

3 dining options (see "Where to Eat," later in this chapter); bikes; children's programs; outdoor pool; bar and store; ice rink in winter; free Wi-Fi. No phone or TV.

Tuolumne Meadows Lodge ★ It may be called a lodge, but it's really just another group of canvas tent-cabins. Like White Wolf Lodge (see p. 87), these have tables and wood-burning stoves and sleep up to four people. The lodge is smack-dab in the middle of prime hiking territory that's less crowded than the valley below, though there is still a fair amount of foot and car traffic here. This is also home base for wilderness trekkers and backcountry campers. Facilities include a tour desk, restaurant, small general store, post office, and stables.

Tioga Rd., Tuolumne Meadows, Yosemite National Park. www.travel yosemite.com. © **801/559-5000.** 69 canvas tent-cabins, all w/shared restrooms and shower facilities. $142 double. Additional $16 per extra adult or $12 per extra child. Parking available in adjacent lot. Closed in winter. From Yosemite Valley, take CA 120 east 60 miles (about 1½ hr.) toward Tioga Pass. **Amenities:** Restaurant (see "Where to Eat," later in this chapter). No phone, TV, or Wi-Fi.

White Wolf Lodge ★ Imagine a smaller, quieter, cleaner Curry Village with larger tents, each equipped with a wood-burning stove. White Wolf Lodge is not a lodge, per se, but a cluster of canvas tent-cabins, with a few wooden cabins out front. It's halfway between the valley and the high country, and generally isn't overrun with visitors. It's a popular spot for midweek hikers and weekend stopovers. Although it can get crowded, it still retains a homey feeling. The wood cabins all have private bathrooms and resemble regular motel rooms, with neat little porches and chairs out front. The canvas cabins beat the Curry Village style by a mile; each can sleep four in a combination of twin and double beds. All have tables, and the helpful staff will show guests how to work the wood-burning stoves.

Tioga Rd., White Wolf, Yosemite National Park. www.travelyosemite. com. © **801/559-5000.** 24 canvas tent-cabins, 4 wood cabins. All canvas cabins share restrooms and shower facilities. $135 tent cabins, $165 wood cabins, $10 per extra adult and $6 per extra child. Parking available across a 2-lane road. Closed in winter. From Yosemite Valley, take CA 120 east 33 miles toward Tioga Pass. **Amenities:** Restaurant (see "Where to Eat," later in this chapter). No phone, TV, or Wi-Fi.

Wawona Hotel ★★   This National Historic Landmark, a classic Victorian-style hotel, is 27 miles from Yosemite Valley and is set near towering trees in an expansive green clearing. The hotel is made of six white clapboard buildings, with the main building constructed in 1879. Don't be surprised if a horse and buggy rounds the driveway by the fishpond—it's that kind of place. What makes it so wonderful? Maybe it's the wide porches, the nearby 9-hole golf course, or the vines of hops cascading from one veranda to the next. Guest rooms are comfortable and quaint; Clark Cottage (dating to 1876) is the most intimate. Live piano music is regularly featured in the lobby.

Wawona Rd., Wawona, Yosemite National Park. www.travelyosemite. com. © **801/559-5000.** 104 units (54 w/shared bathroom); $151 double w/shared bathroom; $224 double w/private bathroom. Lower winter rates. Additional $13–$21 for extra adults. From Yosemite Valley, take CA 41 south 27 miles toward Fresno. **Amenities:** Restaurant (see p. 86); lounge; golf course; large outdoor pool; outdoor tennis court. No phone, TV, or Wi-Fi.

INEXPENSIVE

Housekeeping Camp ★   A fun and funky place to spend the night, this is the closest thing to camping without pitching a tent. The sites are fence-enclosed, canvas-roofed, cinder-block cabins built on concrete slabs. Each is equipped with a table, cupboard, electrical outlets, shelves, mirror, and lights. The sleeping areas have two single-size bunks and a double bed. There is a grocery store on the premises.

Yosemite Valley, Yosemite National Park. www.travelyosemite.com. © **801/559-5000.** 266 units, all w/shared restrooms and shower facilities. $95 per site (up to 4 people; $5 per extra person). Closed Nov to Mar. Parking available or take the shuttle bus to stop no. 12. **Amenities:** No phone, TV, or Wi-Fi.

Outside the Park

The two most important routes into Yosemite are Hwy 120 and Hwy 140. Each is west of the park and home to historic towns that offer a wide range of places to stay, some of which are less expensive than lodging within the park.

ALONG CALIFORNIA 120 & GROVELAND (WEST OF THE PARK)

Visitors approaching from Sacramento, San Francisco, or other regions north of Yosemite usually use Hwy 120, entering the park through the Big Oak Flat gate. Charming little

Groveland, 22 miles from the entrance, is the gateway city here; it's a fun and funky frontier-style town with lots of historic character.

Expensive

Rush Creek Lodge ★★★   New hotels are a rarity in the Groveland area, where many properties are vintage buildings dating to the 1800s. Now there's a new player in the area. Rush Creek, a contemporary hillside resort complex, offers a fresh take on the Yosemite experience. The hotel is only ½ mile from Yosemite's Big Flat entrance (22 miles from Groveland) and provides easy access to the park. Families can find recreation programs and activities at the attractive resort, too, including a gold panning stream, fly-casting pond, and solar-heated saltwater pool. You won't find a TV in your room—hotel management thinks it detracts from the natural environment—but you will find Wi-Fi and an Amazon Echo to play tunes for you. Rooms also have decks or patios, many facing the setting sun.

34001 Hwy 120, Groveland, CA 95321. www.rushcreeklodge.com. ℂ **209/379-2373.** 143 units. $255–$430 double. Lower winter rates. **Amenities:** Heated pool; programs; Jacuzzi; free Wi-Fi.

Moderate

Evergreen Lodge ★   A short drive from the Big Oak Flat entrance, this rustic lodge was originally created as a rough-and-tumble Prohibition-era destination for the workers who built the dam that flooded nearby Hetch Hetchy Valley. The lodge, which recently renovated public areas, features rockers on the decks and porches, forests dotted with play areas for kids, and in-room board games. There's space for two to six guests per cabin, plus "Custom Camping" sites, with tents and all the necessary gear. The lodge's recreation program includes guided bike rides and hikes, live music, Frisbee golf, and s'mores at the campfire.

33160 Evergreen Rd., Groveland, CA 95321. www.evergreenlodge. com. ℂ **209/379-2606.** 88 units, plus 1 private house and 15 custom camping sites. $175–$446 double; $115 campsite. 2-night minimum on weekends and during the summer. Lower winter rates (no camping in winter). **Amenities:** Restaurant (American); bar; bikes; spa; free Wi-Fi. No TVs.

Groveland Hotel ★★   Take a step back in time at the Groveland, one of the grand dames of California Gold Country.

The hotel, listed on the National Register of Historic Places, was built in 1849. Many rooms are named after women of the Sierra and local characters, including Lyle's Room, which honors the hotel's resident ghost. New owners recently remodeled the complex, eliminating the Victorian look and furnishings in favor of sophisticated ranch decor. Standard rooms are spacious, with feather beds, antiques, down comforters, and plush robes. Suites have large spa tubs and fireplaces.

18767 Main St, Groveland, CA 95321. www.groveland.com. © **209/ 962-4000.** 18 units, including 4 suites. $199–$275 doubles; $299– $350 suite. Extra person $20. Lower winter rates. Pets accepted ($20/ night). **Amenities:** Restaurant (See **Provisions Taproom & Bourbon Bar,** p. 89); free Wi-Fi.

Hotel Charlotte ★ Travelers can savor the past at the Charlotte, which reflects the Gold Rush–era background of Groveland. Listed on the National Register of Historic Places, the hotel was built in 1918 by an Italian immigrant of the same name. It's warm, comfortable, and a good choice for those who enjoy the ambience of small historic hotels. Cheerily wallpapered and wainscoted, the guest rooms are small, quaint, and nicely maintained. Several units adjoin each other and have connecting bathrooms (perfect for families) with claw-foot tub/showers.

18736 CA 120, Groveland, CA 95321. www.hotelcharlotte.com. © **800/ 961-7799** or 209/962-6455. 13 units. $149–$325 double. Lower winter rates. **Amenities:** Bar; restaurant; free Wi-Fi.

Yosemite Rose ★ If you like Victorian furniture and design, you might enjoy this B&B on the outskirts of Groveland. It borders Stanislaus National Forest, is 18 miles to Yosemite National Forest; and is close to rafting on the Tuolumne River. Set on a working ranch, this faux Victorian is a product of the 21st century: Built in 2000, the inn was modeled after the Mountain View, California, home of Henry Rengstorff, the 19th-century owner of what is now known as Silicon Valley real estate. A good many of the furnishings here have interesting stories behind them: For example, the Scelestia Room's antique Danish headboard has the face of a demon in the grain; it's supposed to ward off evil spirits. Also on the premises: a three-bedroom ranch house that can sleep up to 12 and a cabin that can sleep six.

22830 Ferretti Rd., Groveland, CA 95321. www.yosemiterose.com. © **866/962-6548.** 7 rooms, including 1 suite, plus 1 cottage and 1 private house. $175–$215 double; $185 suite; $220 cabin; $325 private house. Two-night minimums sometimes required. Rates include full breakfast. **Amenities:** Free Wi-Fi; no TV.

Yosemite Westgate ★   This family-friendly rural lodge is a good place to stay if you can't find lodging within the park. It's 12 miles from the Big Oak Flat entrance to the park and 35 miles to Yosemite Valley. The attractive two-story facility is comfortable and clean with large rooms but is more practical than fancy. There's a playground for kids and a large outdoor pool. No smoking, no pets allowed. The hotel is set in a forested area where you may see wildlife.

7633 Hwy 120, Groveland, CA 95321. www.yosemitewestgate.com. ℂ **800/253-9673** or 209/962-5281. 48 rooms, including some with hot tubs. $189–$259 double. Amenity fee of $5. Lower rates in winter. **Amenities:** Heated pool; laundry facilities; playground; restaurant; free Wi-Fi.

ALONG CALIFORNIA 140 & MARIPOSA
Visitors approaching from San Francisco often use Hwy 140, a scenic route that meanders through Merced River Canyon, a popular spot for river rafting. Mariposa, about halfway between Merced and Yosemite, is one of the largest towns near the park. It has plenty of Western character and offers diverse accommodations, including some well-maintained budget hotels and inexpensive restaurants.

Expensive
Yosemite View Lodge ★   This Merced River lodge is just outside the park's Arch Rock Entrance, and offers nice accommodations with views of the river and surrounding high cliffs. Rooms feature fireplaces, private decks or patios, kitchenettes, and showers for two; several have big jetted tubs. The Yosemite View's sister property, **Yosemite Cedar Lodge,** is just 8 miles down the road, with similar accommodations and slightly lower rates. Just beyond Cedar Lodge are the **Yosemite Resort Homes** at the historic Savage's Trading Post, nicely appointed vacation homes with full kitchens that sleep up to 12, with rates from $300 to $600 a night.

11136 CA 140 (P.O. Box D), El Portal, CA 95318. www.yosemiteresorts.us. ℂ **800/321-5261** or 209/379-2681. 336 units. $209–$269 double; $399–$499 suite. **Amenities:** 2 restaurants; lounge; 5 outdoor Jacuzzis and 1 indoor whirlpool; 3 outdoor pools and 1 indoor pool; Wi-Fi $10 per day.

Inexpensive

Mariposa Lodge ★ The landscaping and ambience are first-rate at this charming motel, which is now part of the America's Best Value Inns' chain. Owned by the Gloor family for three generations, the lodge is on Mariposa's main drag and is reliable and well-maintained. It has grown from one building to three over the years, with smaller rooms in the original structure and larger rooms in the newer two. The most spacious have mission decor and impressive vanities; many also have private balconies. Landscaping is superlative for a roadside motel, especially the garden courtyard around the pool.

5052 CA 140 (P.O. Box 733), Mariposa, CA 95338. www.mariposa lodge.com. ② **800/966-8819.** 45 units. $69–$209 double. Lower winter rates. **Amenities:** Jacuzzi; pool; free Wi-Fi.

River Rock Inn ★ New owners Stephanie and Keith Erikson have worked hard to update Mariposa's oldest motel, which dates back to 1941. Each of the small rooms has been uniquely decorated and is now comfortably chic. The property is small, but you'll be a 3-minute walk from Mariposa County's Old Stone Jail and 10 minutes from Mariposa Museum and History Center. At the River Rock Inn and Cafe, guests enjoy breakfasts of pastries, fresh fruit, and strong coffee; it's also open for breakfast and lunch Monday through Friday.

4993 7th St., Mariposa, CA 95338. www.riverrockncafe.com. ② **209/966-5793.** 9 units. $159–$189 double. Lower winter rates. Continental breakfast is included. **Amenities:** Restaurant; A/C; TV; fridge (in some); no phone; free Wi-Fi.

Yosemite Bug Rustic Mountain Resort & Spa ★★ This folksy oasis in the almost non-existent town of Midpines started out as a hostel in 1996, but it grew and grew, and is now much, much more. The place has something for everybody, with accommodations that range from dorm rooms and tent-cabins to delightful private rooms, plus a good restaurant, a spa, and loads of personality. Surrounded by forest, most of the units have woodsy views that will make you feel like you're in the national park. The dorm rooms are basic, with bunk beds, heat, air-conditioning, individual lockable storage boxes, and conveniently located communal bathrooms and kitchen. The tent-cabins have wooden floors and framing, and various bed combinations, including family units with one double and two single beds; some are heated,

WHERE TO STAY & EAT IN YOSEMITE

some are not. Private rooms have themes, from Western to hippie. Perhaps the best feature of all is the idyllic swimming hole right down the slope from the main lodge, especially on those dog days of summer.

6979 CA 140 (P.O. Box 81), Midpines, CA 95345. www.yosemitebug. com. ℂ **866/826-7108** or 209/966-6666. 64 hostel beds, 16 private rooms w/bathroom, 8 private rooms w/shared bathroom, 16 tent-cabins, 1 studio, 1 private house. Hostel beds $28–$38 per person; private room w/bathroom $95–$175 for 2–5 people; private room w/ shared bathroom $75–$135 for 2–5 people; tent-cabin $40–$85; studio/private house $195–$360. Lower winter rates. **Amenities:** Restaurant (see **June Bug Cafe** on p. 89); Jacuzzi; sauna; spa; free Wi-Fi. No phones.

ALONG CALIFORNIA 41 & OAKHURST

If you're headed to Yosemite National Park from Los Angeles or other parts of Southern California, you'll probably take Hwy 99 through the Central Valley to Fresno, then drive north through the foothills to Oakhurst. It lacks the Western charm of Mariposa and Groveland, but there are enough businesses here to force competition, which means you may find less expensive lodgings. Still, it is difficult to find a room here under $150 in peak summer season; bargain hunters should look to stay in Fresno or Madera en route to Yosemite. Also, remember the distance from Oakhurst into Yosemite Valley: 50 miles on curvy roads, meaning the drive time is about 90 minutes.

Expensive

Auto Camp Yosemite ★★ High-end camping, also called glamping, has arrived in the forest just outside Yosemite National Park. Auto Camp, a hillside park near the Southern Entrance to Yosemite, has 102 accommodations, mostly shiny Airstream trailers, but a few tents and cottages, too. All are tricked out to give campers a taste of luxury, with tile baths and kitchens, communal firepits, a hammock grove, and a two-story clubhouse with a heated pool. There's also a natural fishpond on the grounds of this pet-friendly trailer park and lots of trails nearby.

6323 CA 140, Midpines CA 95345. autocamp.com/guides/location/ Yosemite. ℂ **888/405-7553** or 209/742-2624. 102 units; including cabins, tents, and 75 Airstreams. Airstreams, cabins, and accessible units $300–$500 per night; tents $200–$300. Rates lower in the off season (late fall–winter). Rates include continental breakfast. **Amenities:** Clubhouse activities; outdoor pool; mountain bikes; yoga classes; market with snacks; beverages and apparel; free Wi-Fi.

Château du Sureau & Spa ★★★ This luxurious European-style hotel is a surprising find in the foothills of Oakhurst. A standout small resort, lavish Château du Sureau may be as close as you can get to France on this side of the Atlantic. The 9,000-square-foot inn has an elegant ambience. Its stylish, uniquely decorated accommodations include the extraordinary Saffron Room, with a king-size ebony-and-ivory bedroom set from 1834; Villa du Sureau, a villa with two elaborately decorated bedrooms; and the Sweet Geranium Room, with a private balcony overlooking sumptuous gardens. There are time-tested details such as fresh fruit and fireplaces and impressive art pieces around every corner. The grounds here are similarly phenomenal—featuring a spa, a bocce court, and a lawn-size chessboard with 3-foot-high pawns—and the restaurant, **Erna's Elderberry House,** is simply sublime.

48688 Victoria Lane (P.O. Box 577), Oakhurst, CA 93644. www.chateau sureau.com. ☎ **559/683-6860.** 11 units, including 1 private house. $385–$585 double; $2,950 private house. Rates include full breakfast. **Amenities:** Restaurant (see **Erna's Elderberry House,** p. 87); outdoor pool; spa; free Wi-Fi. No phones; TV on request.

Tenaya Lodge at Yosemite ★★★ Top-rated Tenaya Lodge continues to upgrade, having spent another $25 million to improve the lodge and its programs. The newest addition: 50 modular stand-alone, two-bedroom Explorer Cabins surrounded by towering sugar pines and incense cedars. The lodge, which seems to have one foot in the Adirondack Mountains and another in the Southwest, is set on 48 acres surrounded by Sierra National Forest and features a wide array of organized year-round recreational activities. The comfortable guest rooms are modern, and the grand lobby has an impressive river-rock fireplace that towers three stories. In addition to the new cabins, guests can also choose the Cottages at Tenaya, duplex units with balconies and fireplaces set off from the main lodge. Other pluses: Ascent Spa, a LEED-certified facility with 12 treatment rooms, and an ice rink, horse-drawn sleigh rides, and sledding hill for winter visitors.

1122 CA 41, Fish Camp, CA 93623. www.tenayalodge.com. ☎ **888/ 775-6680** or 559/683-6555. 352 units, including 249 rooms and suites, 53 cottages and 50 two-bedroom cabins. Summer rates: $339–$499 lodge rooms or cottages; $445–$899 suite or cabin. Resort fee is $30 a day. Lower winter rates. Children stay free in parent's room. Buffet breakfast $30 per couple. Pets accepted ($100 fee). **Amenities:** 5 restaurants; exercise room; 1 indoor pool; 3 outdoor pools; room service; spa; free Wi-Fi.

Moderate

The Homestead ★   Secluded on 40 acres of woodland with plenty of trails, this off-the-beaten-path establishment is a gem. The delightful cottages here are rustic yet modern, with four-poster log beds, Saltillo tile floors, stone fireplaces, and separate sitting and dining areas, plus TV, air-conditioning and Wi-Fi. Each unit has its own unique bent, from the romantic Garden Cottage to the cozy Star Gazing Loft to the two-bedroom Ranch House (the most family-friendly option here). There's also a community BBQ area.

41110 Rd. 600, Ahwahnee, CA 93601. www.homesteadcottages.com. ☎ **559/683-0495.** Drive 4½ miles north of Oakhurst on CA 49, then south on Rd. 600 for 2½ miles. 7 cottages, $179–$359 double. **Amenities:** Free Wi-Fi.

Hounds Tooth Inn ★   This Victorian-style inn is a good choice for those who want easy access to Yosemite from the south side but desire more intimacy than a motel or sprawling resort can offer. Set a few hundred feet from the highway, the off-white inn houses a dozen similar guest rooms, each with modern conveniences as well as antique reproductions and in-room sinks. There's also a private summer house (850 sq. ft.) with a king-size bed, kitchenette, Jacuzzi, and private patio. The garden area is perfect for whiling away an evening in peace and quiet. Breakfast and wine and cheese appetizers served daily.

42971 CA 41, Oakhurst, CA 93644. www.houndstoothinn.com. ☎ **888/642-6610** or 559/642-6600. 13 units, including 1 cottage. $195–$500 double; $250–$700 cottage. **Amenities:** Movie library; free Wi-Fi.

ALONG U.S. 395 (LEE VINING)

If you're planning to access Yosemite National Park from the east, you'll need to use Hwy 395, which skirts the banks of Mono Lake, then enters Lee Vining. Gas up, eat and sleep here before catching Hwy 120 to the park. Lee Vining is about 12 miles from Yosemite's Tioga Pass entrance. Remember, this route is only open during the summer.

Inexpensive

El Mono Motel ★ Built in the 1920s, this artfully renovated European-style lodging is our pick on the east side of the park in Lee Vining. Fronted by attractive porches and a barbecue area, the guest rooms feature vibrant color schemes and down comforters; the only drawbacks are their small size and the fact that some of them share bathrooms. But all in all, this eclectic lodging is a perfect place to bunk after an expedition in Tuolumne Meadows. The property is also home to a good deal of local art, a coffeehouse/bakery, and organic garden.

51 U.S. 395, Lee Vining, CA 93541. www.elmonomotel.com. ℂ **760/647-6310.** 11 units (6 w/shared bathroom). $79–$139 double. Closed Nov to late May. **Amenities:** Restaurant; free Wi-Fi. No phone, no TV, no A/C.

Lake View Lodge ★ Located just a half-mile from Hwy 120, the route to Tioga Pass, this cheerful motel is spread across several green lawns populated by birds and butterflies. It's reliably clean, with well-maintained rooms and cottages set off from the main highway. The former features one king or queen bed or two queens and the latter sleeps up to eight people.

51285 U.S. 395, Lee Vining, CA 93541. www.lakeviewlodgeyosemite.com. ℂ **760/647-6543.** 46 units, including 16 cottages. $149–$189 double; $109–$359 cottage. **Amenities:** Free Wi-Fi.

CAMPING

There are numerous camping opportunities both within and surrounding Yosemite National Park. Brief descriptions of individual campgrounds follow; you'll find additional details in the campground chart on p. 134.

Note: When camping in this area, proper food storage (bear-proof canisters or lockers) is *required* for the sake of the black bears in the parks, as well as for your safety. See local bulletin boards for instructions.

Inside the Park

There are 13 campgrounds, and nearly 1,500 campsites in Yosemite National Park, some 400 of which are in Yosemite Valley. Campsite reservations are required for most. Reservations are accepted beginning on the 15th of each month and can be made up to 5 months in advance; make your reservations (www.recreation.gov; ✆ **877/444-6777**) as soon as possible, especially for sites in the valley. Find tips for navigating the process at www.nps.gov/yose/planyourvisit/nrrs.htm. Unless noted otherwise, pets are accepted at all the following campgrounds. Additional campground information is available at ✆ **209/372-0200.**

Wilderness permits are required for all overnight backpacking trips in the park, whether you decide to use an established campsite or pick out your own camping area. No wilderness camping is allowed in the valley. For more information on wilderness camping, including Yosemite's High Sierra Camps, see "Hikes & Other Outdoor Pursuits in Yosemite," p. 109.

The busiest campgrounds in the park are in Yosemite Valley. All four of the following campgrounds are in the valley and have flush toilets and access to the showers nearby at Half Dome Village. **Upper Pines Campground ★** is pretty and shady, but you won't find peace and quiet here in the summer. Parking is available, or you can take the shuttle bus to stop no. 15 or 19. **Lower Pines Campground ★** is wide open, with lots of shade but limited privacy. Still, it's a nice place with clean bathrooms, and it's bordered on the north by a picturesque meadow. Parking is available, or take the shuttle bus to stop no. 19. **North Pines Campground ★★** is beautifully situated beneath a grove of pine trees that offers lots of shade but little privacy. The campground is near the river, roughly a mile from Mirror Lake. Parking is available, or take the shuttle bus to stop no. 18. Reservations are required for Upper, Lower, and North Pines campgrounds. **Camp 4 ★** (also called Sunnyside Walk-In) has tent sites only. It's a small campground that's become a magnet for hikers and climbers taking off on or returning from trips. It's situated behind Yosemite Lodge, near the trail head for Yosemite Falls, and close to rocks frequently used by novice rock climbers. Pets are not permitted. Parking is available about 150 feet away, or take the shuttle bus to stop no. 7.

Elsewhere in the park, **Bridalveil Creek Campground ★★**, at Glacier Point, is set along Bridalveil Creek, which flows to Bridalveil Fall—a beauty of a waterfall, especially after a snowy winter or wet spring. Located near stunning Glacier Point, and featuring flush toilets, this campground is away from the valley crowds but still within a moderate drive to the valley sights. The campground can accommodate some pack animals; call for information. Take CA 41 (from either direction) to Glacier Point Road. The campground is about 8 miles down the road.

Several campgrounds are in the vicinity of the Big Oak Flat Entrance, roughly 20 to 25 miles from Yosemite Valley. **Hodgdon Meadow Campground ★**, which has RV and tent sites, including some walk-in sites, requires reservations April through October but is first come, first served the rest of the year. It has flush toilets and is located about 1 mile inside the entrance along North Crane Creek and near the Tuolumne River's South Fork. The Big Trees are 3 miles southeast. **Crane Flat Campground ★**, a large, pleasant campground with flush toilets, is located on Big Oak Flat Road near the Tioga Road turnoff. **Tamarack Flat Campground ★** is a bit off the beaten path and, therefore, more secluded than most, which means fewer folks rest their heads here. Equidistant from Yosemite Valley and Tuolumne Meadows, it has pit toilets, does not allow pets, and is not suitable for large RVs or trailers. Take Tioga Road east from Big Oak Flat Road about 3 miles and turn right onto the access road. The campground is another 3 miles down the road. Reservations are not available, first-come, first-served.

Options in the White Wolf area include **Porcupine Flat Campground ★**, which offers lots of shade, shrubs, and trees, although facilities are pretty much limited to pit toilets. You have a chance of finding a spot here if you're in a pinch. Pets are not permitted. It's located near Yosemite Creek along Tioga Road, 16 miles west of Tuolumne Meadows and 38 miles east of Yosemite Valley. First-come, first-served. **White Wolf Campground ★**, secluded in a forest, is a generally delightful campground where you might want to spend several days. It has flush toilets and offers easy access to nearby hiking, with trails that lead to several lakes, including Grant Lake and Lukens Lake. On the downside, mosquitoes make their presence felt here in summer. From Big Oak Flat Road, turn east onto Tioga Road, drive 15 miles to White Wolf Road, and turn left. The road dead-ends at the campground. First-come, first-served.

Among Yosemite's other camping opportunities is **Tuolumne Meadows Campground ★★**, the biggest in the park and, amazingly, often the least crowded. Its location in the high country makes it a good spot from which to head off with a backpack. The site is also near the Tuolumne River, making it a smart choice for anglers. In addition to standard RV/tent sites, the campground has 25 walk-in spaces for backpackers and eight group sites; half of the sites require reservations. There are flush toilets, and showers are available (for a fee) at nearby Tuolumne Lodge. From Big Oak Flat Road, head east on Tioga Road for about 45 miles to Tuolumne Meadows.

Wawona Campground ★★, which requires reservations April through September (but is open year-round), has flush toilets and can accommodate pack animals; call for information. There's not much seclusion here, but the location, shaded beneath towering trees, is beautiful. The campground is near the Mariposa Grove of giant sequoias and is also close to the Merced River, which offers some of the better fishing in the park. The campground is about 1 mile north of Wawona.

Yosemite Creek Campground ★, in a pretty setting along Yosemite Creek, has pit toilets and little else in terms of facilities, and no potable water, but sometimes has sites available when the park's other campgrounds are full. From Big Oak Flat Road, head east on Tioga Road for about 30 miles and turn right on the access road. The campground is 5 miles down the road.

Outside the Park

Yosemite is surrounded by national forests that offer campgrounds comparable to the ones in the park, although often less developed and less crowded. There are also private campgrounds, which usually provide level sites, complete RV hookups, hot showers, coin-operated laundries, convenience stores, and other amenities.

WEST ALONG CALIFORNIA 120

The following campgrounds, located along CA 120 west of Yosemite National Park, are all in the Stanislaus National Forest's **Groveland Ranger District** (www.fs.usda.gov/recarea/stanislaus/recreation; ℂ **209/962-7825**). They all have vault toilets and can accommodate rigs up to 22 feet long.

Lumsden Campground ★ is located along the Tuolumne River, on a scenic stretch between the Hetch Hetchy and Don Pedro reservoirs. The campground offers fishing in a primitive

Yosemite Campgrounds

CAMPGROUND	ELEV. (FT.)	TOTAL SITES	RV HOOKUPS	DUMP STATION
INSIDE YOSEMITE NATIONAL PARK				
Bridalveil Creek	7,200	110	0	No
Camp 4	4,000	35	0	No
Crane Flat	6,191	166	0	No
Hodgdon Meadow	4,872	105	0	No
Lower Pines	4,000	60	0	Nearby
North Pines	4,000	81	0	Nearby
Porcupine Flat	8,100	52	0	No
Tamarack Flat	6,315	52	0	No
Tuolumne Meadows	8,600	304	0	Nearby
Upper Pines	4,000	238	0	Yes
Wawona	4,000	93	0	Nearby
White Wolf	8,000	74	0	No
Yosemite Creek	7,659	75	0	No
OUTSIDE THE PARK				
Big Bend	7,800	17	0	No
Ellery Lake	9,500	21	0	No
Jerseydale	4,000	10	0	No
Junction	9,600	13	0	No
Lost Claim	3,100	10	0	No
Lumsden	1,500	10	0	No
Lumsden Bridge	1,500	9	0	No
The Pines	3,200	11	0	No
Saddlebag Lake	10,000	20	0	No
South Fork	1,500	8	0	No
Summerdale	5,000	29	0	No
Summit	5,800	6	0	No
Sweetwater	3,000	12	0	No
Tioga Lake	9,700	13	0	No
Yosemite–Mariposa KOA	2,400	89	51	Yes

setting but can get unbelievably hot in the summer. From Groveland, take CA 120 about 7½ miles east to Ferretti Road, turn left and drive about 1 mile to Lumsden Road, turn right at Lumsden Road, and travel about 6½ miles on a steep, narrow dirt road to the campground. **Lumsden Bridge Campground ★** is about 1½ miles past Lumsden Campground (on Lumsden Rd.). Set in a pine and oak forest along the Tuolumne

TOILETS	DRINKING WATER	SHOWERS	FIRE PITS/ GRILLS	LAUNDRY	RESERVATIONS POSSIBLE	FEES	OPEN
Yes	Yes	No	Yes	No	No	$14	July–early Sept
Yes	Yes	Nearby	Yes	Nearby	No	$5	All year
Yes	Yes	No	Yes	No	Yes	$20	July–mid-Oct
Yes	Yes	No	Yes	Yes	May–Sept	$20	All year
Yes	Yes	Nearby	Yes	Nearby	Yes	$20	Late Mar–Oct
Yes	Yes	Nearby	Yes	Nearby	Yes	$20	Late Mar–mid-Oct
Yes	No	No	Yes	No	No	$10	July–mid-Oct
Yes	No	No	Yes	No	No	$10	July–mid-Oct
Yes	Yes	Nearby	Yes	No	Yes	$20	July–Sept
Yes	Yes	Nearby	Yes	Nearby	Yes	$20	All year
Yes	Yes	No	Yes	Yes	May–Sept	$20	All year
Yes	Yes	No	Yes	No	No	$14	July–mid-Sept
Yes	No	No	Yes	No	No	$10	July–Sept
Yes	Yes	No	Yes	No	No	$19	Late Apr–mid-Oct
Yes	Yes	No	Yes	No	No	$19	June–mid-Oct
Yes	Yes	No	Yes	No	No	Free	May–Nov
Yes	No	No	Yes	No	No	$14	June–Oct
Yes	Yes	No	Yes	No	No	$16	May–Labor Day
Yes	No	No	Yes	No	No	Free	All year
Yes	No	No	Yes	No	No	Free	Mid-Apr–Oct
Yes	Yes	No	Yes	No	No	$16	All year
Yes	Yes	No	Yes	No	No	$19	June–mid-Oct
Yes	No	No	Yes	No	No	Free	Mid-Apr–Oct
Yes	Yes	No	Yes	No	Yes	$20	June–Nov
Yes	No	No	Yes	No	No	Free	June–Oct
Yes	Yes	No	Yes	No	No	$19	Apr–Oct
Yes	Yes	No	Yes	No	No	$19	June–mid-Oct
Yes	Yes	Yes	Yes	Yes	Yes	$40–$50	Mid-Mar–late Oct

River, it is a favorite of rafters because the location is close to some of the Tuolumne River's best, and most scenic, stretches of white water. **South Fork Campground ★**, also located along Lumsden Road near Lumsden and Lumsden Bridge campgrounds, is a pretty spot just off the Tuolumne River. Trailers or vehicles with low ground clearance should not be taken to any of the above three campgrounds.

The **Pines Campground** ★ is about 9 miles east of Groveland via CA 120, and although it's in a mixed conifer forest, it can get very hot in the summer. Drinking water is available only in the summer. **Lost Claim Campground** ★, about 12 miles east of Groveland via CA 120, offers easy access on a paved road. There are some trees and the river nearby. Drinking water is supplied by a hand pump. Trailers are not recommended. **Sweetwater Campground** ★, 15 miles east of Groveland on CA 120, is a pretty option in a mixed conifer forest with many shady sites, but it also gets hot in summer.

ALONG CALIFORNIA 140

Jerseydale Campground ★, situated in the Sierra National Forest (www.fs.fed.us/r5/sierra; ✆ **559/297-0706**), provides refuge from the crowds and makes a great base for exploring the area. There are vault toilets and hiking trails, and you can get to the Merced River via a nearby trail head. From Mariposa, drive about 12 miles northwest on CA 49 to Jerseydale Road, which leads to the campground and adjacent Jerseydale Ranger Station.

A small Bureau of Land Management facility, **McCabe Flat Campground** ★, is located along the Merced River. Tables and grills can be found in the shade of oak and pine trees. Bring your own drinking water. From Mariposa, travel north on Highway 140, 11.8 miles, turn left at Briceburg Visitor Center. Drive over the Briceburg Bridge, travel 2.3 miles to the campground. Vault toilets, no reservations. For more information visit www.fs.fed.us/r5/sierra or call ✆ **209/966-3192.**

ALONG CALIFORNIA 41

Two Sierra National Forest campgrounds (see contact information for Jerseydale Campground, above) offer pleasant camping, with vault toilets, in a woodsy atmosphere along CA 41 southwest of Yosemite. **Summerdale Campground** ★ is about a mile north of Fish Camp via CA 41, on the South Fork of the Merced River, and is often full by noon on Fridays; reservations are available through **www.recreation.gov**.

EAST ALONG CALIFORNIA 120

The Inyo National Forest operates small, attractive campgrounds along CA 120 east of the national park. These include **Big Bend Campground** ★, 7 miles west of Lee Vining via CA 120. Located on the eastern Sierra along Lee Vining Creek, this campground is sparse but has breathtaking views of towering

Camping

WHERE TO STAY & EAT IN YOSEMITE

cliffs. It has vault toilets. **Ellery Lake Campground** ★, which also has vault toilets, is at scenic Ellery Lake, about 9 miles west of Lee Vining via CA 120. **Junction Campground** ★ is near Ellery and Tioga lakes, with easy access to the Tioga Tarns Nature Trail. Set among pines at 9,600 feet, most of the 13 campsites are shaded. Sites 1–5 can accommodate RV's or multiple vehicles with a maxim parking length of 40 ft. It has vault toilets and is 10 miles west of Lee Vining along CA 120.

At 10,000 feet, **Saddlebag Lake Campground** ★ is among the highest-elevation drive-to campgrounds in the state. It's situated along Saddlebag Lake and near Lee Vining Creek. The campground is a beautiful place that's worth staying at and exploring for a while. It's also a great base for those who want to head out into the wilderness with a backpack. Vault toilets are available. From Lee Vining, drive 10 miles west on CA 120; then turn north on Saddlebag Lake Road and go about 2 miles to the campground. **Tioga Lake Campground** ★, another high-elevation campground, is a pretty place to camp and has vault toilets. From Lee Vining, drive 10 miles west on CA 120.

Information on these U.S. Forest Service campgrounds is available from the **Mono Basin Scenic Area Visitor Center,** located on the west shore of Mono Lake (✆ **760/647-3044**), and the **Inyo National Forest,** 351 Pacu Lane, Ste. 200, Bishop, CA 93514 (www.fs.fed.us/r5/inyo; ✆ **760/873-2500**).

WHERE TO EAT

Yosemite National Park restaurants aren't generally known for their culinary prowess, except for the Ahwahnee Hotel Dining Room, the Mountain Room Restaurant, and Wawona Hotel. But the setting is wonderful, so it's easy to forgive a boring menu. There are plenty of dining possibilities in and near the park, so you certainly won't go hungry. However, you won't find many bargains, so be sure to bring a full wallet with your empty stomach.

In the Valley
EXPENSIVE
Ahwahnee Dining Room ★★★ AMERICAN/CONTINENTAL   Even if you're a happiest-when-sleeping-under-the-stars backpacker, you'll be impressed by the Ahwahnee's dining room. This is where the great outdoors meets upscale

cuisine, and it's a wonderful place to celebrate a special occasion. The cavernous room, its candelabra chandeliers hanging from the 34-foot-high beamed ceiling, seats 300 diners who have wonderful views of Yosemite Valley through 24-foot windows. Massive timbered walls give the place a look straight out of medieval Great Britain. The menu changes frequently and offers a good variety of creative dishes, steaks, seafood, prime rib, pasta. There's also a nice Sunday brunch. An extensive wine list, featuring selections from California and abroad, is offered at lunch and dinner. Breakfast includes French toast, hotcakes, omelets, and eggs benedict. Lunch choices include sautéed trout, a spicy pulled pork sandwich, fettuccine pesto Alfredo, and a variety of plates and salads. Sunday brunch is a big event.

Note: The dinner dress code requires men to wear a collared shirt and long pants and women to wear a dress, skirt, or pants with a blouse. But breakfast and lunch are casual, in case you didn't pack for a formal dinner.

Ahwahnee Dining Room. www.travelyosemite.com. © **209/372-1489.** Reservations required for dinner. Breakfast $7–$21; lunch $15–$23; dinner $30–$49; Sun brunch $56 adults, $2.50 children. Mon–Sat 7–10:30am, 11:30am–3pm, and 5:30–9pm; Sun 7am–3pm and 5:30–9pm. Shuttle-bus stop no. 3.

MODERATE

Mountain Room Restaurant ★ AMERICAN   The best thing about this restaurant is the view. The food's excellent, too, with an emphasis on local organic ingredients, but the floor-to-ceiling windows overlooking Yosemite Falls are simply spectacular—and there's not a bad seat in the house. We suggest the steaks and the salmon, but there are many dishes to choose from, including a Portobello mushroom entrée. Meals come complete with vegetables and bread. There are also vegetarian and gluten-free dishes, as well as a nice dessert tray. It's got a good wine list, too. The **Mountain Room Lounge** features an open-air fireplace and an a la carte menu.

Yosemite Valley Lodge, Yosemite Valley. www.travelyosemite.com. Main courses $7–$40. Daily 5–9pm. Shuttle-bus stop no. 8.

INEXPENSIVE

Base Camp Eatery ★ INTERNATIONAL   This renovated food court, renamed to honor the rock climbers and mountaineers of Yosemite, serves breakfast, lunch, and dinner.

There's also a Starbucks now, delighting coffee lovers. The Eatery is set up with kiosks, where you can order on a screen, or at the counter, then pick up your choices before heading to a table either indoors or at the outside seating area, which features tables with umbrellas and good views of Yosemite Falls. The food stations specialize in Italian food, offering pizza, calzones, and pasta; grilled food and sandwiches with fast-food favorites; and Asian foods, such as noodles and salads. There are also desserts, baked goods, and beverages. In the morning, look for a hot breakfast station offering traditional American breakfast items.

Note: Base Camp Eatery is located near the center of Yosemite Lodge, which is a great central location if you're staying at the lodge or visiting the valley. Parking in Yosemite Valley can be tight, but the lodge usually has ample parking

Yosemite Valley Lodge, Yosemite Valley. Main courses $8–$15. Daily 6:30am–9:30pm. Shuttle-bus stop no. 8.

Degnan's Kitchen ★ DELI   Pizza, burgers, and sandwiches are the main offerings at this Yosemite Village cafe. But you can also get soups, chili, and breakfast. Customers order on screen at kiosks, then pick up breakfast, lunch, or dinner at counters. Sometimes the ordering lines are long, but they usually move quickly. In addition to the sandwiches, there is a variety of prepared items and drinks to carry off for a day on the trail. You'll also find a selection of fruit drinks, beer, and wine.

Yosemite Village, Yosemite Valley. Most items $3–$11. Daily 7am–6pm. Shuttle-bus stop nos. 4 and 10.

Degnan's Loft ★ INTERNATIONAL   This cheery restaurant, with a fireplace and beamed ceilings, is adjacent to Degnan's Kitchen (see above). Choose from Mexican fare, Asian rice bowls, and pizza. The Loft also offers a good atmosphere to catch a game on big flatscreen TVs.

Yosemite Village, Yosemite Valley. Main courses $8–$15. Hours 11:30am–9pm. Closed in winter. Shuttle-bus stop nos. 4 and 10.

Meadow Grill ★ AMERICAN   If you're in the vicinity of Half Dome Village, you find a variety of sandwiches, burgers, hot dogs, and grab-and-go salads here. It's a good place for a quick bite.

Half Dome Village, Yosemite Valley. Most items $3–$10. 11am–8pm. Closed in winter. Shuttle-bus stop nos. 13, 14, and 20.

Pavilion ★ AMERICAN   A good spot for the very hungry. All-you-can-eat breakfast and dinner buffets offer a wide variety of well-prepared basic American selections at reasonable prices.

Half Dome Village, Yosemite Valley. Range $4–$15, daily 7–10am and 5:30–8:30pm. Shuttle-bus stop nos. 13, 14, and 20.

Pizza Patio ★ PIZZA   Another Half Dome Village eatery, Pizza Patio offers large umbrellas, table service, and a great view of Glacier Point, plus or minus a hundred kids. The bar also taps a few brews, plus cocktails. This is a great place to chill after a long day.

Half Dome Village, Yosemite Valley. Pizza $9–$21 Summer daily 11am–10pm; shorter winter hours. Shuttle-bus stop nos.13, 14, and 20.

Village Coffee Corner ★ COFFEE SHOP   Specialty coffees and fresh-baked pastries are the fare here. You can also get ice cream and shakes after 11am.

Half Dome Village, Yosemite Valley. Most items $2–$7. Summer daily 6am–11pm; shorter winter hours. Shuttle-bus stop nos.13, 14, and 20.

Village Grill ★ AMERICAN   This seasonal Yosemite Village eatery is a fast-food joint that's a decent place to pick up a quick bite. It offers burgers, chicken sandwiches, veggie dishes, and the like, and has outdoor seating.

Yosemite Village, Yosemite Valley. Most items $3–$10. Daily 11am–6pm. Closed in winter. Shuttle-bus stop nos. 2, 10.

Elsewhere in the Park
MODERATE
Wawona Dining Room ★★ AMERICAN   The dining room at the Wawona Hotel is wide open, with lots of windows, sunlight, and views of towering trees. It's a Victorian jewel, with lovely sequoia-painted lamps lighting the old-fashioned, white-tablecloth dining room. During the summer, you can also dine outside on the wide porch that lines the front of the hotel. Dinners are flavorful, with pot roast a specialty of the house. In addition, choose from dinner entrees such as honey-glazed chicken, New York steak, and stuffed trout. "Tasteful, casual attire" is requested for those having dinner at the hotel, but the dress code loosens up for those having breakfast or lunch. Burgers, pasta, salads, and

sandwiches are available at lunch, and breakfast fare such as eggs and pancakes are available in the morning.

At Wawona Hotel, Wawona Rd. www.travelyosemite.com. ℂ **209/ 375-1425.** Lunch $7–$12; dinner main courses $11–$33. Breakfast 7am–10am, lunch 11am–3pm, dinner 5–9pm.

White Wolf Lodge ★ AMERICAN   The changing menu in this casual restaurant offers a variety of standards served up in generous portions. Breakfast choices include eggs, pancakes, omelets, or biscuits and gravy; dinner always features beef, chicken, fish, pasta, and vegetarian dishes. Takeout lunches are also available from noon to 2pm.

White Wolf, Tioga Rd. ℂ **209/372-8416.** Breakfast buffet $12, child $6.25; dinner 4-course $36, $10 children. 7:30–10:30am and 5:30–8pm.

INEXPENSIVE
Tuolumne Meadows Lodge ★ AMERICAN   One of the two restaurants in Yosemite's high country, this lodge offers something for everyone. The breakfast menu features the basics, including eggs, pancakes, fruit, oatmeal, and granola. Dinners always include a beef, chicken, fish, pasta, and vegetarian specialty, all of which change frequently.

Tuolumne Meadows, CA 120. ℂ **209/372-8413.** Reservations required for dinner. Breakfast $4–$13; dinner main courses $13–$30. Daily 7–9am and 5:30–8pm.

Outside the Park

In the mood for a mocha latte or a lavender cookie? Stop by Groveland's **Mountain Sage,** where you can get a bite to eat, sip a cup of coffee or tea, pick up a hiking stick, buy a T-shirt or cap, check your e-mail, and relax in a hammock all in one place. The facility, a converted home, also has a nursery in the back and sells local art. Look for the popular coffeehouse in Groveland at 18653 Main St. (ℂ **209/962-4686**).

EXPENSIVE
Erna's Elderberry House ★★★ EUROPEAN/NEW AMERICAN   The elegant restaurant at Château du Sureau is a surprising find in the foothills near Yosemite: It is an international award winner, consistently scoring high marks for its cuisine and ambience. The menu, which changes nightly, is a fusion of European and California culinary traditions. Offerings might include marinated mussels and chilled

carrot-coconut soup; pan-seared Tasmanian sea trout with oatmeal crust; prosciutto-wrapped beef tenderloin; spinach gnocchi; and blueberry-yogurt terrine. Each menu lists recommended wines to complement the evening's entrees. A dress code stipulates men wear a button-down shirt and slacks and women wear "casual dressy" attire. Founder Erna Kubin-Clanin, who owned the hotel and dining room for more than 33 years, sold the facility in 2017.

At Château du Sureau & Spa, 48688 Victoria Lane, Oakhurst. www. elderberryhouse.com. *©* **559/683-6800.** Reservations recommended. Seven-course tasting menu is $145 per person. Daily 5:30–8:30pm; Sun also 11am–1pm.

MODERATE

Charles Street Dinner House ★★ AMERICAN   This friendly and warm dining room is locally famous for its steaks, honey-baked ribs, and New Zealand rack of lamb. Portions are large and savory. At least one seafood dish is available nightly. The restaurant is in a historic 1800s building and features decor straight out of the Old West, with a huge wagon wheel in the front window and nice touches such as family photos and fresh flowers. Service is excellent. Open for lunch and dinner.

5043 Charles St. (CA 140), Mariposa. www.charlesstreetdinnerhouse. net. *©* **209/966-2366.** Reservations recommended. Main courses $20–$34. Open daily 5–9:30pm.

Charlotte Tavern ★ NEW AMERICAN   You'll find California-centric Southern comfort food at this historic hotel's small dining room. A variety of seasonal specials is offered in addition to small plates such as asparagus fries and slow-roasted pork belly bites. The menu fluctuates depending on produce and meat available from local farmers.

At the Hotel Charlotte, 18736 CA 120, Groveland. www.hotelcharlotte. com. *©* **209/962-6455.** Reservations recommended. Main courses $10–$23. Thurs–Mon, 5:30–8:30pm.

Iron Door Saloon & Grill ★ AMERICAN   In 1852, this family-friendly establishment started serving whiskey from an obligatory "plank over two flour barrels," making it California's oldest bar. Now it's the colorful anchor to a city block of businesses (including a soda fountain and a general

Where to Eat

WHERE TO STAY & EAT IN YOSEMITE

store), with scads of dollar bills hanging from the ceiling alongside rusted mining equipment, a menagerie of taxidermy, and odd little displays on such topics as the origin of Groveland's name and the career of Black Bart. The menu is basic, listing steaks and burgers and poultry, as well as fresh fish and pasta. You can eat in the 150-year-old bar or the adjacent dining room, which is more upscale with tiled floors, rock walls, and historical photographs. Lunch features sandwiches and salads (plus floats and shakes from the soda fountain). The food and service don't quite live up to the colorful atmosphere, but the Iron Door is a can't-miss nonetheless.

18761 CA 120, Groveland. ✆ **209/962-6244.** Lunch $12–$20; dinner main courses $15–$30. Mon–Sun 7am–10pm Bar stays open later.

June Bug Cafe ★★ AMERICAN   Ask the Mariposa locals for their favorite place to get a great meal at a reasonable price, and it will likely be this bustling eatery. It's a noisy, busy restaurant at the Yosemite Bug Rustic Mountain Resort. The casual space contains several rooms with knotty-pine walls, oak floors, wooden chairs and tables, and an open-beamed ceiling. You order at a counter and your food is delivered to your table. The innovative American dishes, with Mediterranean and Californian influences, emphasize organic ingredients, many from an on-site garden. Each night features different offerings: You might have top sirloin, a trout filet with lime butter, or stuffed Portobello mushrooms. There is at least one vegetarian and one vegan option at every meal. Breakfasts here range from bacon and eggs to buckwheat pancakes or granola; lunches include sandwiches and sack lunches to go.

At the Yosemite Bug Rustic Mountain Resort & Spa, 6979 CA 140, Midpines. www.yosemitebug.com. ✆ **209/966-6666.** Breakfast and lunch items $5–$10; dinner main courses $9–$18. Daily 7am–9pm.

Provisions Taproom & Bourbon Bar ★ AMERICAN You'll find music, libations, and small plates at this lounge in a restored 1849 Adobe taproom at the Groveland Hotel. On draft, there are 10 craft beers, hard cider, and prosecco; there is also a wide selection of local wines and more than 30 bourbons, whiskeys, and scotch. The food selection includes charcuterie and cheese boards, veggies, panini, and other light dishes. Summer season features courtyard dining as well as regularly scheduled concerts under the stars.

At the Groveland Hotel, 18767 CA 120, Groveland. www.groveland. com. ℰ **800/273-3314** or 209/962-4000. Small plates $8–$16. Summer daily 5:30–9pm; shorter winter hours.

Savoury's ★★ NEW AMERICAN   The dining room is sleek, spare, and stylish here, decorated with nature photos and art. Savoury's is chic but casual and features excellent service and simple, fresh dishes. Among your choices: chipotle-pesto chicken, spicy shrimp diablo, vegan and vegetarian dishes, and hand-cut steaks. For dessert, dig into a decadent panna cotta on a bed of strawberry sauce or the addictive lemon mousse.

5034 Charles St. (CA 140), Mariposa. ℰ **209/966-7677.** Main courses $18–$42. Hours: 5–9pm.

Whoa Nellie Deli ★ DELI/NEW AMERICAN   What looks to be an ordinary gas station is home to a truly extraordinary eatery that serves thousands of people on summer days. Inside the Tioga Gas Mart—aka "The Mobil"—Chef Matt "Tioga" Toomey offers some of the most tantalizing plates in the Sierra Nevada, as well as plump to-go sandwiches and pizzas. Take a seat in a booth or on the popular patio and enjoy your breakfast or lunch before moving on. The menu includes fish tacos with mango salsa and ginger slaw, pork tenderloin with apricot-berry glaze, and wild-buffalo meatloaf with garlic mashers. We especially like the lobster and crab taquitos with tomatillo salsa—and the transcendent chocolate cake. All plates overflow with excellent salads and heaps of fresh fruit, making the deli the best post-backpacking eatery in the area.

CA 120, just west of U.S. 395, Lee Vining. www.whoanelliedeli.com. ℰ **760/647-1088.** Breakfast and lunch $5–$16; dinner main courses $11–$23. Daily 7am–8pm. Closed Nov–Apr.

INEXPENSIVE

Castillo's Mexican Food ★★ MEXICAN   Established in 1955, this cozy cantina serves heaping portions of well-prepared Mexican favorites. Entrees come with salad, rice, and beans, and can also be ordered a la carte. A house specialty, the *tostada compuesta,* fills a hungry belly with your choice of meat, plus beans, lettuce, and cheese, stuffed into a bowl-shaped crisp tortilla and topped with avocado and sour cream. Various combo plates are available, or you can choose from several steak specialties and seafood dishes such as jumbo shrimp fajitas. For those who like a little extra fire, there's *camarones a la diabla*—shrimp sautéed in butter, garlic, and crushed red chiles. The garden seating is our favorite spot here.

4995 5th St., Mariposa. © **209/742-4413.** Reservations recommended in summer. Lunch and dinner main courses $6–$17. Daily 11am–9pm.

Happy Burger Diner ★ AMERICAN   One of the best fast-food joints in the region, the Happy Burger offers practically any type of fast food you can think of, with everything cooked fresh to order. The food here takes a few minutes longer than at your usual chain restaurant, but it's worth it. Breakfast (served until 11:30am) includes numerous egg dishes, French toast, pancakes, oatmeal, and the like. The lunch and dinner menu, available all day, features a multitude of charbroiled burgers, sandwiches, stuffed potatoes, Mexican dishes, salads, and dinner plates such as top sirloin and fried shrimp.

In typical fast-food restaurant style, you place your order at the counter and your piping-hot meal will then be delivered to your booth, where you'll sit among record album covers from the '60s and '70s and a vintage pinball game.

5120 Charles St. (CA 140) at 12th St., Mariposa. www.happyburger diner.com. © **209/966-2719.** Most items $6–$15. Daily 6am–9pm.

Pete's Place ★ GREEK/AMERICAN   A local institution in Oakhurst, this diner does a good job with Greek and American staples, especially during breakfast, with options such as egg dishes and pancakes. For lunch, there are burgers and gyro sandwiches.

40093 CA 410, Oakhurst. © **559/683-0772.** Breakfast and lunch main courses $10–$15. Open 7am–3pm daily.

Picnic & Camping Supplies

If you forget something, chances are, you'll be able to get it in the national park's bustling Yosemite Valley, though it's tough to find equipment elsewhere in the park. In the valley, the best place to pick up supplies and camping equipment is the **Yosemite Village Store,** which stocks groceries, clothing, and maps; it also has an ATM. Unfortunately, it also has long lines much of the time. Be patient when you shop there. The **Yosemite Lodge Gift Shop** and **Curry Village Gift & Grocery** stock some supplies. The **Mountain Shop** in Curry Village sells clothing and equipment for rock climbs, day hikes, and backcountry excursions, while the **Tuolumne Meadows Store & Mountain Shop** also carries backpacking supplies, including maps and dehydrated food. The **Badger Pass Ski Area Sport Shop** (open only during the snow season) stocks ski clothing and other winter supplies. There are also several small convenience stores located throughout the park.

In Mariposa, you'll find a good selection of groceries plus a deli at **Pioneer Market,** 5034 Coakley Circle (🕾 **209/742-6100**), behind the town rest area. In Oakhurst, our choice for a grocery store is **Raley's,** 40041 CA 41 (🕾 **559/683-8300**). In El Portal, just outside the park's Arch Rock Entrance, you'll find the well-stocked **El Portal Food Market,** on CA 140 (🕾 **209/379-2440**), featuring good coffee, pastries, and premade sandwiches. On the east side of the park in Lee Vining, the upscale **Mono Market** (🕾 **760/647-1010**) can't be beat if you're in search of natural and organic foods.

EXPLORING SEQUOIA & KINGS CANYON

Although Sequoia & Kings Canyon National Parks are larger than Yosemite, they receive less than half as many visitors annually. But the two parks—just 75 miles from Yosemite—are dazzling, offering one of the deepest canyons in North America, some of the largest trees in the world, and Mt. Whitney, the tallest mountain in the lower 48 states. Most of the land in these side-by-side parks is wilderness, best explored on foot. But travelers in a hurry will find excellent roads that will deliver them to the parks' highlights: rugged foothills, huge mountains, deep canyons, vast caverns, and the world's largest trees, able to live 3,000 years and grow as tall as a 26-story building. Short trails help complete the picture. The crowds are thinner here, although travelers can still expect slow traffic in the summer. Free shuttles help ease congestion.

ESSENTIALS

Access/Entry Points

From the west, access the Big Stump Entrance (Kings Canyon National Park) via CA 180, and the Ash Mountain Entrance (Sequoia National Park) via CA 198. Continuing east on CA 180 also brings you to an entrance near Cedar Grove Village in the canyon itself, which is open only in summer. See the "Sequoia & Kings Canyon National Parks" map (p. 4) and the "Highway

Marmot Invasion
Always do a quick check under your hood before leaving a parking lot. Marmots, especially in the Mineral King area, love munching on car hoses and wiring, leaving a trail of disabled vehicles in their wake. A good number of them have stowed away in a car's engine compartment and hitched rides with unsuspecting drivers to other parts of the parks; several have ridden as far as Los Angeles.

Access to the Parks" map (inside front cover) to orient yourself. To access the Mineral King area of Sequoia National Park, take the steep, twisting Mineral King Road (closed in winter) off CA 198, just a few miles outside the Ash Mountain Entrance.

Visitor Centers & Information

The parks have three major visitor centers open year-round, some seasonal facilities, and a museum. Make one of these facilities your first stop so you can buy books and maps and discuss your plans with park rangers. Call ℂ **559/565-3341** or visit **www.nps.gov/seki** for information.

In Sequoia National Park, the largest visitor center is **Foothills Visitor Center** (ℂ **559/565-4212**), just inside the Ash Mountain Entrance on CA 198. Exhibits here focus on the Sierra Foothills, a biologically diverse ecosystem.

About 15 miles farther on CA 198 is the **Giant Forest Museum** (ℂ **559/565-4480**), housed in a historic building and offering extensive exhibits on giant sequoias.

Lodgepole Visitor Center (ℂ **559/565-4436**) includes exhibits on geology, wildlife, air quality, and park history. It's located 4½ miles north of Giant Forest Village. The center is closed weekdays in winter, but it may be open on weekends.

In Kings Canyon National Park, the **Kings Canyon Visitor Center,** in Grant Grove (ℂ **559/565-4307**), includes exhibits on logging and the role of fire in the forests.

Open in summer only are Kings Canyon's small **Cedar Grove Visitor Center** (ℂ **559/565-3793**) and Sequoia's **Mineral King Ranger Station** (ℂ **559/565-3768**), where you can get backcountry permits and information.

Fees

It costs $35 per motor vehicle ($20 per individual on foot, bike, or motorcycle) to enter the park for up to 7 days. Camping fees range from $14 to $23 a night in the park. The Sequoia & Kings Canyon yearly pass, which allows unlimited entry into the park but does not cover camping fees, sells for $70. Also see "Special Permits & Passes," p. 171.

Regulations

In Sequoia & Kings Canyon, there is a 14-day camping limit from June 14 to September 14, with a maximum of 30 camping days per year. Check campsite bulletin boards for additional regulations. Some campgrounds close in winter (see the chart on p. 134). Pets are allowed in campgrounds, but they must be on a leash and are not allowed on any trails.

The most important warning in Sequoia & Kings Canyon, which cannot be repeated too often, is that this is **bear country,** and proper food storage is required for the safety and health of both visitors and the resident black bears. In addition, rattlesnakes are common, so be careful where you put your feet and hands. In the Foothills area, check your clothes frequently for ticks; poison oak is another hazard.

The roads in the park are particularly steep and winding. Those in RVs will find it easiest to use CA 180 from Fresno.

ORIENTATION

The parks are roughly equidistant—5 hours by car—from both San Francisco and Los Angeles. Kings Canyon National Park borders Sequoia National Park on the north and is nearest to Yosemite and Fresno. Kings Canyon contains the developed areas of Grant Grove and Cedar Grove. Sequoia National Park is home to the Giant Forest sequoia grove, as well as Lodgepole, the Foothills, and Mineral King. The main entrance (for all except Mineral King) is on CA 198 (which becomes Generals Highway in the parks), via Ash Mountain through Visalia and Three Rivers. From Sequoia's border, Visalia is 36 miles and Three Rivers is 7 miles.

Although it's impossible to drive through the parks from west to east—the High Sierras get in the way—the north–south Generals Highway connects Grant Grove in Kings Canyon National Park with Giant Forest in Sequoia National

Park. The highway runs 25 miles between two giant sequoias named for famous American generals—the General Grant Tree and the General Sherman Tree. Allow at least an hour to drive between the two on this slow, winding route—not including delays for construction, planned for the foreseeable future. From several miles inside the CA 198 Ash Mountain Entrance to Giant Forest, Generals Highway is narrow and winding and not recommended for vehicles over 22 feet long, which should enter the parks from CA 180.

The road to Mineral King turns south off CA 198 about 3 miles east of Three Rivers, crosses private and public land, and heads 11 miles to the Lookout Point Entrance. From here it's another 15 miles to Mineral King. This steep, narrow, twisting, dead-end road is closed in winter and does not connect with any other park roads, which puts the Mineral King area off-limits to motor vehicles during the winter and well into spring.

Introducing Sequoia National Park

The best-known stand of sequoias in the world can be found in **Giant Forest,** part of Sequoia National Park. Named in 1875 by explorer and environmentalist John Muir, this area consists mostly of huge meadows and a large grove of trees. At the northern edge of the grove, you can't miss the **General Sherman Tree,** considered the largest living tree on the planet, although it is neither the tallest nor the widest. Its size is noteworthy because of the tree's mass—experts estimate the weight of its trunk at about 1,385 tons. The General Sherman Tree is 275 feet tall; it measures 102½ feet around at its base, and its largest branch is 6¾ feet in diameter. It is

A Question of Size

In the past, the National Park Service claimed that the General Sherman Tree is the largest living thing on earth. Technically, however, this may not be quite true, and now the claim is that it's the largest living tree, still quite a distinction. The reason for the change? Park officials say it has been discovered that some underground fungi may actually be bigger than the General Sherman Tree. In addition, there are groves of aspen trees in the Rockies that share a common root system and may be considered one living thing, thereby exceeding the General in overall size.

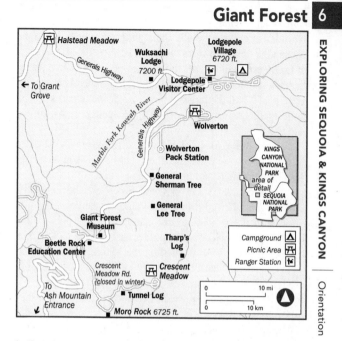

believed to be about 2,100 years old—*and it's still growing.* Every year, it adds enough new wood to make another 60-foot-tall tree. The tree is part of the 2-mile **Congress Trail,** a foot trail that includes groups of trees with names such as the Senate and the House. Also in the area is the **Beetle Rock Education Center,** a fun place for kids to investigate science and nature.

Another interesting stop in Giant Forest is **Tharp's Log,** a cabin named after the first non–Native American settler in the area, Hale Tharp, who grazed cattle among the giant sequoias and built a summer cabin in the 1860s from a fallen sequoia hollowed by fire. It is the oldest cabin remaining in the park.

Pretty **Crescent Meadow** is a pristine clearing dotted with wildflowers and tall grasses. A trail (described in "The Highlights" section, p. 103) wraps around the meadow. This is also the trail head for several backcountry hikes.

Also in the area is **Moro Rock,** a large granite dome well worth the half-hour climb up and back. From the top, Moro Rock offers one of the most spectacular views of the dark and barren Great Western Divide, which includes the Kaweah Range. The divide is one of two crests in the southern Sierra Nevada but is not officially the main crest, which lies to the east and is obscured from view.

Lodgepole Village, the most developed area in both parks, lies just northeast of Giant Forest on the Generals Highway. Here you'll find the largest visitor center in the parks, plus a large market, several places to eat, a laundry, a post office, and showers.

Nearby, the **Wuksachi Village & Lodge** replaced older facilities that were damaging the Giant Forest sequoia grove. There's a dining room, gift shop, and lodge.

About 16 miles south of Giant Forest are the **Foothills.** Located near the Ash Mountain Entrance, the Foothills area offers a visitor center, several campgrounds, a picnic area, and **Hospital Rock,** a large boulder with ancient pictographs believed to have been painted by the Monache Indians who once lived here. Nearby are about 50 grinding spots probably used to smash acorns into flour. A short trail leads down to a serene place along the Kaweah River where the water gushes over rapids into deep, clear pools.

Mineral King, in the southern part of the park, is a pristine high-mountain valley carved by glaciers and bordered by the tall peaks of the Great Western Divide. Red and orange shale mix with white marble, black metamorphic shale, and granite to give the rocky landscape a rainbow of hues. This area resembles the Rocky Mountains more than the rest of the Sierra Nevada because the peaks are formed of metamorphic rock. A silver prospector gave Mineral King its name in the 1800s, and the region was annexed to the park in 1978. The trails in Mineral King begin at 7,500 feet and climb. To reach the area, head west from the Ash Mountain Entrance 3 miles on CA 198 to the turnoff—watch for the sign. Then it's a daunting 28-mile trip that makes around 700 tight turns and takes 1½ hours. Trailers, RVs, and buses are not allowed. The road is closed in winter, when the area is prone to avalanches.

Introducing Kings Canyon National Park

Of the three Central California parks, Kings Canyon is the least visited, although it offers the serenity that many hikers seek. Its rugged canyons, soaring mountains, and desolate

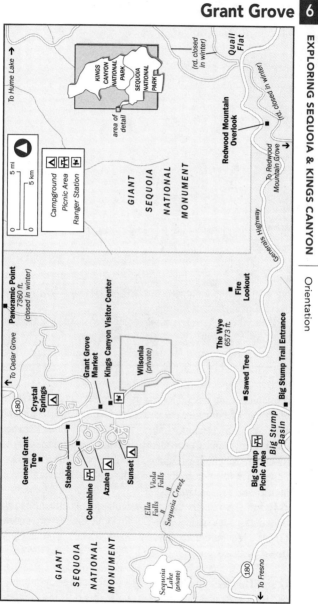

KINGS
CANYON
NATIONAL
PARK

SEQUOIA
NATIONAL
PARK

area of detail

Quail Flat

(rd. closed in winter)

Redwood Mountain Overlook ■

(rd. closed in winter)

To Redwood Mountain Grove →

Generals Highway

▲ Campground
🏕 Picnic Area
👤 Ranger Station

0 — 5 mi
0 — 5 km

GIANT
SEQUOIA
NATIONAL
MONUMENT

Panoramic Point
7360 ft.
(closed in winter)

↑ To Cedar Grove

Fire Lookout ■

Grant Grove Market

Kings Canyon Visitor Center

Wilsonia
(private)

The Wye
6573 ft.

Sawed Tree ■

Big Stump Trail Entrance ■

Crystal Springs
(180)

General Grant Tree

Stables

Columbine 🏕

Azalea ▲

Sunset ▲

Viola Falls

Ella Falls

Sequoia Creek

Big Stump Picnic Area 🏕

Big Stump Basin

GIANT
SEQUOIA
NATIONAL
MONUMENT

Sequoia Lake
(private)

(180)

↓ To Fresno

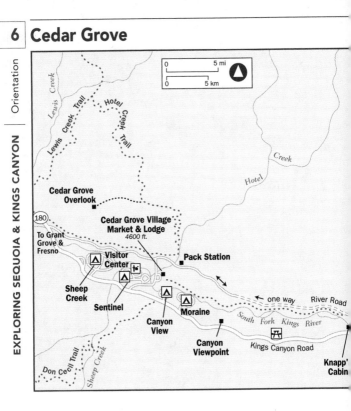

backcountry are a hiker's paradise. The park includes **Grant Grove** and **Cedar Grove,** as well as portions of the Monarch Wilderness and Jennie Lakes Wilderness. *Note:* Between Grant Grove and Cedar Grove is **Giant Sequoia National Monument,** which is managed as part of Sequoia National Forest. This region includes Hume Lake, Boyden Cavern, and several campgrounds.

Grant Grove is the most crowded region in either Sequoia or Kings Canyon. Here you'll find the towering **General Grant Tree** amid a grove of spectacular giant sequoias. The tree was discovered by Joseph Hardin Tomas in 1862 and named 5 years later by Lucretia P. Baker to honor Ulysses S. Grant. The tree measures 267½ feet tall, has a circumference of 107½ feet, and is thought to be the world's third-largest living tree, possibly 2,000 years old, just a youngster in this neighborhood. It was officially declared the "Nation's

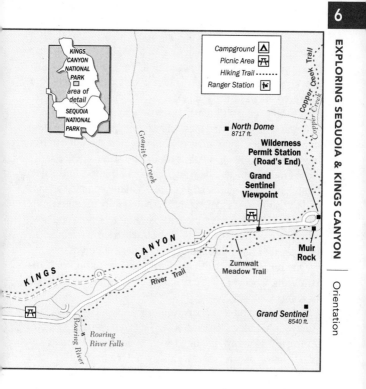

Christmas Tree" by President Calvin Coolidge in 1926 and remains the centerpiece of an annual Christmas tree ceremony.

Two and a half miles southwest of the grove is **Big Stump Trail,** an instructive hike that can be depressing as it winds among the remains of logged sequoias. Since sequoia wood decays slowly, you'll see century-old piles of leftover sawdust that remain from the logging days. In summer, visitors can drive a short distance to **Panoramic Point,** stand atop this 7,520-foot ledge, and look across a long stretch of the Sierra Nevada for a glimpse of Kings Canyon.

Cedar Grove, 35 miles east, may be in the same park although it seems a world away. While Grant Grove is usually crowded, Cedar Grove seems off the beaten path. That this region still exists is sheer luck. There were once plans to flood Kings Canyon by damming the Kings River, a decision that would have buried Cedar Grove beneath a deep lake. Today that's considered an inconceivable move. With the flood threat abated, the region stood to become another Yosemite, but people fought hard to avoid the overcrowding and development that had occurred in Yosemite, and eventually everyone agreed it was better to keep development to a minimum. It was finally annexed in 1965 and, under a master plan for the area, will remain as it is today.

Cedar Grove is abundant with lush foliage, crashing waterfalls, and miles upon miles of solitude. Half the fun of driving through Kings Canyon is seeing its sheer granite walls close around you and the wild South Fork of the Kings River tumble by. The small **Cedar Grove Village** contains a store and gift shop, restaurant, laundry, showers, lodge, and campgrounds. This region of the park is often less crowded than others. Remember that it is also closed from November to mid-April or later, depending on weather conditions.

One mile east of the Cedar Grove Village turnoff is **Canyon View,** where visitors can see the glacially carved U-shape of Kings Canyon.

Easily accessible nature trails in Cedar Grove include Zumwalt Meadow, Roaring River Falls, and Knapp's Cabin. **Zumwalt Meadow** is dotted with ponderosa pine and has good views of two rock formations: **Grand Sentinel** and **North Dome.** The top of Grand Sentinel is 8,504 feet above sea level, while North Dome, which some say resembles Half Dome in Yosemite, tops out at 8,717 feet. The mile-long trail around the meadow is one of the prettiest in the park. The best place to access this walk is at a parking lot 4½ miles east of the turnoff for Cedar Grove Village.

Roaring River Falls is a 5-minute walk from the parking area, 3 miles east of the turnoff to Cedar Grove Village. Even during summers and dry years, the water here crashes through a narrow granite chute into a cold green pool below. During a wet spring, these falls are powerful enough to drench visitors who venture too close. **Knapp's Cabin** can be reached via a short walk from a turnoff 2 miles east of the road to Cedar Grove Village. Here, during the 1920s, Santa Barbara businessman George Knapp commissioned lavish fishing expeditions and used this tiny cabin to store his expensive gear.

The **Monarch Wilderness** is a 45,000-acre region protected under the 1984 California Wilderness Act. Part of it lies on the grounds of Sequoia National Forest, adjoining the wilderness in Kings Canyon National Park. It's tough to reach and so steep that hikers practically need to be roped in to climb. You're close to the wilderness area when you pass Kings Canyon Lodge and Boyden Cavern.

The **Jennie Lakes Wilderness** is smaller, at 10,500 acres. Although it's possible to hike through in a day, it exhibits a variety of wilderness features, including the 10,365-foot Mitchell Peak and several wide lowland meadows. This region lies between the Generals Highway and CA 180, east of Grant Grove. About 7 miles southeast of Grant Grove, Big Meadows Road (closed in winter) takes off from Generals Highway and heads east into Sequoia National Forest. From this road, you can access several trails that lead into Jennie Lakes Wilderness.

THE HIGHLIGHTS

The view atop **Moro Rock** is one of the most spectacular in the Sierra—the Great Western Divide dominates the eastern horizon. These high-elevation barren mountains can seem dark and ominous, even though snow caps the ridge line throughout the year. The cliffs appear towering and steep, and with some peaks over 13,000 feet, they are only slightly below the summit of Mount Whitney (14,505 ft.), which is obscured from view. The climb to the top of the Rock takes you up hundreds of stairs, so pace yourself. The summit offers a narrow, fenced plateau with endless views. During a full moon, the mountain peaks shimmer like silver. See "Seeing the Parks by Car & Shuttle," p. 107.

Mist Falls is a wide, powerful waterfall accessible only on foot (see p. 117), but the trek is well worth the effort. The waterfall is especially impressive during spring and early summer, when it's fed by snowmelt, and the cascading water crashing onto the rocks below drowns out most other sounds. This is also when you're likely to see rainbows.

Crescent Meadow is a large, picturesque clearing dotted with high grass and wildflowers, and encircled by a forest of firs and sequoias. The park's oldest cabin is along this route as well. This is a particularly nice hike in early morning and at dusk, when the low-angle sunlight allows for the best photography (see p. 110).

A Nearby National Monument

Some of the most beautiful scenery in the Sequoia & Kings Canyon National Parks area is not actually in either of these national parks, but in an adjacent section of the Sequoia National Forest that was designated a national monument at the start of this century.

Now covering 353,000 acres, **Giant Sequoia National Monument** was created by President Bill Clinton in 2000. The monument contains 38 groves of sequoias, including some of the most magnificent giant trees to be seen anywhere. In addition, it has towering domes of granite; scenic **Hume Lake,** a popular destination for boaters and anglers; and the spectacular **Kings Canyon**—the deepest canyon in North America, with elevations ranging from 1,000 to 11,000 feet. Expect this magnificent canyon to be inaccessible by car in the winter months.

Among the hiking trails in the monument is the **Boole Tree Trail,** a moderate 2.5-mile loop trail that leads to Boole Tree, the largest sequoia in the 1.1-million-acre Sequoia National Forest and the eighth-largest tree in the world. This trail, located off Forest Road 13S55, off Kings Canyon Highway, includes forest and open country, where you'll see sequoias, scenic vistas of the Kings River, and wildflowers in summer.

An easy walk on the quarter-mile (one-way) **Chicago Stump Trail** leads to the stump of the General Noble Tree, which was cut down, chopped into pieces, and then reassembled and displayed at the 1893 World's Fair in Chicago. Some fairgoers refused to believe that a tree could grow so big and dubbed it "the California hoax."

Information about other attractions and facilities within the monument, such as the beautiful drive through Kings Canyon and the underground world of Boyden Cavern, are discussed elsewhere in this book.

Primitive camping is allowed and there is no fee. For additional information on Giant Sequoia National Monument, contact the **Hume Lake Ranger District,** Sequoia National Forest, 35860 E. Kings Canyon Rd. (CA 180), Dunlap, CA 93621 (© **559/338-2251**).

Exploring the Inside of the Earth

There are more than 275 caves in the Sequoia & Kings Canyon National Parks area, but only two are open for tours by the general public—one in Sequoia National Park and the other in Giant Sequoia National Monument, just outside Kings Canyon National Park.

South of the Giant Forest in Sequoia National Park is the turnoff from the Generals Highway for **Crystal Cave,** a beautiful underground world that was formed from limestone that turned to marble. The cave contains an array of cave formations, many still growing, that range from sharply pointed stalactites and towering stalagmites to elaborate flowing draperies. To reach the entrance, drive 7 miles down the narrow winding road (RVs, trailers, and buses are prohibited), and walk 0.5 miles down a steep path to the cave. *Note:* To take a tour, you need to get advance tickets, available at www.recreation.gov and at both the Lodgepole and Foothills visitor centers.

The Sequoia Natural History Association conducts 45-minute **guided tours** along paved, lighted pathways. The tours are offered from mid-June to Labor Day daily every half-hour from 10:30am to 4:30pm, from mid-May to mid-June and after Labor Day to late October daily every hour from 11am to 3pm (with slightly longer weekend hours). The cost is $16 for adults, $15 for seniors 65 and older, and $8 for children 5 to 12 (free for children under 5). A special **discovery tour** is offered in summer only, Monday through Friday at 4:15pm. It is less structured and limited to 18 people, has a minimum age requirement of 13, and costs $25 per person. There is also a belly-crawling **wild cave tour** ($140, 4–6 hr.) on Saturdays in summer. The cave is a constant 48°F (9°C), so take a sweater or jacket. Sturdy footwear is recommended, and strollers, tripods, and backpacks are prohibited. Information is available at visitor centers or by telephone (www.sequoia parksconservancy.org/crystalcave.html; *©* **559/565-4251**).

Ten miles west of Cedar Grove, in Giant Sequoia National Monument, is **Boyden Cavern,** the only other cave in the area that hosts tours. Boyden is an especially scenic cave known

---

Impressions

It is in this cave [Crystal Cave] that nature has lavishly traced her design in decorative glory.
                                                        —Park Superintendent Walter Fry, 1925

for a wide variety of formations, including rare "shields," which consist of two roughly circular halves of mineral deposits that look like flattened clam shells. Highlights include a flowstone formation, known as Mother Nature's Wedding Cake, and the appropriately named Christmas Tree and Baby Elephant formations. The cave is open daily from late May through mid-November. Hours are usually 10am to 5pm in June, but often are shorter at the beginning and end of the season. Visitors get to see the cave on guided 50-minute tours that follow a well-lit, handrail-equipped trail. Tours leave approximately every hour on the hour. The cost is $16 for ages 13 and up, $8 for children 5 to 12; $5 for children 4 and younger. Reservations can be made at https://boydencavern. com. Private walking tours are also available for $30, with a four-person minimum. Guides will take you and your group on a private tour—move at your own pace, take extra time for photographs, and enjoy the cavern in a smaller group setting. For information, contact **Boyden Cavern** (https://boyden cavern.com; ✆ **888/965-8243**).

SEEING THE PARKS IN 1 OR 2 DAYS

Eighty percent of the parks' visitors come here on day trips—an amazing statistic, considering the geography of this place. It takes 3 to 4 days to do the parks justice, but it is possible to take a short walk through a grove of big trees in an afternoon. Day-trippers should stick to **Grant Grove,** if possible—it's the most accessible. Coming from the south, Giant Forest is a good alternative, although the trip takes a while on the steep and narrow Generals Highway. **Cedar Grove** and **Mineral King,** two other destination points, are farther afield and require an early start or an overnight stay.

If you have only 1 day, we recommend driving from the Foothills through Giant Forest to Grant Grove, or vice versa. It's about 2 hours through the park, plus whatever additional time is necessary to resume your route outside its entrances. Start at a park visitor center—there's one near each location—to get your bearings. Whether traveling from the north or south, you'll see the varied terrain within the park as you pass through dense forest, exposed meadows, and scrubby foothills covered in oaks and underbrush. In spring and summer, much of the route may be dotted with wildflowers. The southern portion runs along the Kaweah River. This route also passes two large stands of giant sequoias: one at Grant Grove and the other at Giant Forest. Both have easy trails looping through the majestic stands. At Grant Grove, a footpath passes lengthwise through a fallen sequoia.

SEEING THE PARKS BY CAR & SHUTTLE

Although these two parks are generally considered the domain of hikers, and they contain only 127 miles of paved roads between them, you will have a use for your car here. Those who don't have the time or energy to lace up a pair of hiking boots and take off down a trail will still be able to enjoy the scenery, often from the comfort of their vehicle or from roadside and near-roadside viewpoints.

The **Generals Highway** runs nearly 50 miles from Sequoia National Park's Ash Mountain Entrance to Grant Grove in Kings Canyon National Park, passing through the Giant Forest, home of the world's largest sequoia trees. It's a beautiful drive, with optional stops to see the Giant Forest Museum and the General Sherman Tree. There are also several easy walking trails along the way (see p. 109 for details). From several miles inside the Ash Mountain Entrance to Giant Forest, Generals Highway is narrow and winding and not recommended for vehicles over 22 feet long.

A VACATION FROM your car

Since 2007, the National Park Service and the City of Visalia have operated a transportation system that makes it possible to explore Sequoia National Park without a car. From Visalia (or Three Rivers), the **Sequoia Shuttle** (www.sequoiashuttle.com; ℂ 877/287-4453) will take you to the Giant Forest Museum for $20 round-trip. From here, riders can connect with the **free park shuttle** to get to Wuksachi Lodge or one of the numerous trail heads en route. The former makes five runs between 6am and 6:30pm daily (reservations are accepted); the latter runs from 9am to 6pm daily. Both shuttles operate in the summer only, although there has been some talk of extending the season; call for current information.

For a short, scenic drive in Sequoia National Park, we recommend the paved **Moro Rock/Crescent Meadow Road,** a 3-mile dead-end road (open in summer only) that runs from the Giant Forest Museum, along the Generals Highway, south and east through a grove of sequoias. Along the way, you can see the fallen sequoia at Auto Log (now too rotted out to support a vehicle), drive through a hollowed-out fallen sequoia at Tunnel Log, and stop for a steep 0.3-mile walk up to the top of Moro Rock for a spectacular panoramic view. This road ends at Crescent Meadow, known for its colorful wildflowers in summer. See also the sections on Moro Rock and Crescent Meadow in "The Highlights," p. 103.

Kings Canyon Highway, from the Grant Grove area to Cedar Grove in Kings Canyon National Park, is a lovely drive of 35 miles, but most of its especially scenic sections are not in the park. Instead, some of the best roadside scenery is in Giant Sequoia National Monument (see "A Nearby National Monument," p. 104). For part of the journey, Kings Canyon Highway (also called CA 180) is high above the Kings River, offering breathtaking vistas of the canyon; then it seems to almost join the river, giving motorists a close-up view of the rapids as the water crashes over and among huge boulders. Well worth a stop along this route are the spectacular Grizzly Falls. Allow about an hour. The eastern two-thirds of this road are open during the summer only.

ORGANIZED TOURS & RANGER PROGRAMS

The Sequoia Parks Conservancy Field Institute (www. sequoiaparks.org/sequoiajourneys; *©* **559/565-4251**) offers tours of Crystal Cave and a wide variety of hikes and activities each season. Tickets for Crystal Cave tours can be bought online at www.recreation.gov. Check their online calendar for up-to-date activities and events.

Ranger programs include free walks and talks at Giant Forest, Lodgepole, Grant Grove, Mineral King, and Foothills. Some of the highlights include weekend wildflower walks at Foothills, talks at General Sherman, and evening campfire programs at Lodgepole. Visit their website at www. nps.gov/planyourvisit or check bulletin boards and visitor centers for the current schedule.

HIKES & OUTDOOR PURSUITS IN SEQUOIA & KINGS CANYON

Take a hike: That's the best way to explore the ancient trees and magical mountains of Sequoia & Kings Canyon parks. There are nearly 1,000 miles of trails, ranging from gentle walks among giant sequoias to moderate day hikes and high-powered ascents (including Mt. Whitney, the highest point in the lower 48 states). More than 85% of the parks' land—nearly a million acres—is designated as wilderness, accessible only to those on foot or horseback. Backcountry visitors see glacial canyons, broad lakes, lush meadows, and sheer granite peaks that combine to form the core of the largest expanse of contiguous wilderness in California.

DAY HIKES & SCENIC WALKS

Although much of Sequoia & Kings Canyon is designated as wilderness, you don't have to be a hardcore backpacker to enjoy the parks. You can see many of their highlights on short walks and day hikes. In many cases, after just 5 minutes on the trail, you'll feel you've left the world's stresses behind. If you choose to venture away from the highway, at almost any point you're likely to find an abundance of natural wonders: colorful flora, interesting fauna, and an incredible landscape created over millions of years. Below, we suggest day hikes that will help you experience the best these parks have to offer. A trail map is helpful; some trail intersections are confusing, and signs can disappear.

Big Trees Trail, the trail to the General Sherman Tree, and Hazelwood Nature Trail are wheelchair accessible, and several trails in the Giant Forest area can be negotiated by wheelchair. See **www.nps.gov/seki/planyourvisit/accessibility.htm** for additional information.

Near Giant Forest

Big Trees Trail ★★ This scenic loop walk among the sequoias skirts a pretty meadow, with trailside exhibits that explain why this area is such a good habitat for sequoias. There are usually abundant wildflowers in Round Meadow in early summer. The trail is wheelchair accessible, paved with some wooden boardwalk sections.

0.7 miles/1 hr. Easy. Start at the Giant Forest Museum.

Congress Trail ★★ This self-guided walk circles some of Sequoia National Park's most well-known and best-loved giants. The trail is a paved loop with a 200-foot elevation gain. Here you'll find the General Sherman Tree, considered to be the largest living tree on earth. The Lincoln Tree is nearby, along with several clusters of trees, including the House and the Senate. Try standing in the middle of these small groups of trees to gain the perspective of an ant at a picnic. The walk is also dotted with inviting benches.

2 miles/1–3 hr. Easy. Start at the General Sherman Tree, just off the Generals Hwy., 2 miles northeast of Giant Forest Museum.

Crescent Meadow Loop ★ The meadow is a large, picturesque clearing dotted with high grass and wildflowers, encircled by a forest of firs and sequoias. The park's oldest cabin (Tharp's Log) is along this paved route as well. This is a particularly nice hike in early morning and at dusk, when the indirect sunlight provides the best photo opportunities.

1.8 miles/1–3 hr. Easy. Begin at the Crescent Meadow parking area.

Hazelwood Nature Trail ★ Follow the signs for a fine walk that winds among several stands of sequoias,

Hikes near Giant Forest

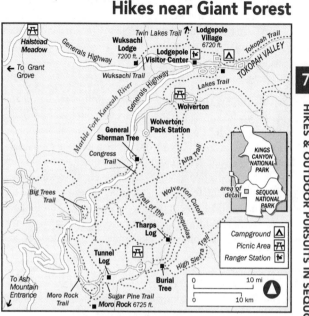

accompanied by exhibits that explain the relationship among trees, fire, and humans. Wheelchair accessible.

1 mile/1 hr. Easy. Begin on the south side of the Generals Hwy., across from the road to Round Meadow.

High Sierra Trail ★★ Although this hike is a gateway to the backcountry, the first few miles of the trail also make a great day hike. Along the way, you'll find spectacular views of the Kaweah River's Middle Fork and the Great Western Divide. The trail runs along a south-facing slope, so it's warm in spring and fall. Get an early start in summer. From the trail head, cross two wooden bridges over Crescent Creek until you reach a junction. Tharp's Log is to the left, with the High Sierra Trail to the right. After hiking 0.8 miles, you'll reach Eagle View, which offers a picturesque vision of the Great Western Divide. On the south side of the canyon are the craggy Castle Rocks. Continue to see Panther Rock, Alta Peak, and Alta Meadow. At 2.8 miles is a sign for the Wolverton Cutoff, a trail used as a stock route between the Wolverton trail head and the high country. A bit farther on, you'll come upon Panther Creek and a small waterfall. At 3.3 miles, you'll see pink-and-gray Panther Rock. Follow a few more creeks to reach the last fork of Panther Creek, running down a steep, eroded ravine.

9 miles/6 hr. Moderate. The trail head is near the restrooms at the Crescent Meadow parking area.

Huckleberry Trail ★★   Look for wildflowers in the summer on this hike, which offers beauty without the crush of too many people. It passes through forests and meadows full of wildflowers, near a 100-year-old cabin, and by an old American Indian village. The first mile of this hike takes you along the Hazelwood Nature Trail (p. 110). Head south at each junction along the way until you see a big sign with blue lettering that marks the start of Huckleberry Trail. You'll pass a small creek and meadow before reaching a second sign to Huckleberry Meadow. The next mile is steep and crosses beneath sequoias, dogwoods, and white firs.

At the 1.5-mile point is Squatter's Cabin, a log building built in the 1880s. East of the cabin is a trail junction. Head north (left) up a short hill. At the next junction, veer left along the edges of Circle Meadow for about 0.3 miles before you reach another junction. On the right is a short detour to Bear's Bathtub, a pair of sequoias hollowed by fire and filled with water. Legend has it that an old mountain guide named Chester Wright once surprised a bear taking a bath here, hence its name. Continue heading northeast to the Washington Tree, which is almost as big as the General Sherman Tree, and then on to Alta Trail. Turn west (left) to Little Deer Creek. On both sides of the creek are American Indian mortar holes. At the next junction, head north (right) to return to the Generals Highway and the last leg of the Huckleberry Trail to the parking area.

5.2 miles/2–3 hr. Moderate. Begin at the Hazelwood Nature Trail parking area, ⅓ mile east of Giant Forest Museum on the Generals Hwy.

Moro Rock ★★★   Heavily trafficked walk climbs 300 feet up 400 steps that twist along this gigantic boulder perched perilously on a ridge top. Take it slowly. The view from the top is breathtaking, stretching to the Great Western Divide, which looks barren and dark, like the end of the world. The mountains are often snowcapped well into summer. During a full moon, the view is even stranger and more beautiful.

0.3 miles/30–60 min. Moderate. Begin at the Moro Rock parking area.

Moro Rock & Soldiers Loop Trail ★ This hike cuts cross-country from the Giant Forest Village to Moro Rock, heading through a forest dotted with giant sequoias. Be advised that a carpet of ferns occasionally hides the trail. It pops out at Moro Rock, and then it's just a quick heart-thumper to the top (see the trail description above).

4.6 miles/3–4 hr. Moderate. The trail head is just west of Giant Forest Museum.

Trail of the Sequoias ★ Expect solitude on this trail that offers a longer, more remote hike into Giant Forest, away from the crowds and along some of the more scenic points of the park. The first 0.3 miles is along the Congress Trail before heading uphill at Alta Trail. Look for signs that read TRAIL OF THE SEQUOIAS. After 1.5 miles, including a 0.5-mile steep climb among giant sequoias, you'll encounter the ridge of the Giant Forest. Here you'll find a variety of trees, young and old, fallen and sturdy. Notice the shallow root system of fallen trees and the lightning-blasted tops of others still standing. The trail continues to Log Meadow, past Crescent Meadow, and to Chimney Tree, a sequoia hollowed by fire. At the junction with Huckleberry Trail, follow the blue and green signs straight (north) toward Sherman Tree and back to Congress Trail.

6 miles/4 hr. Moderate. The trail head is at the northeast end of the General Sherman Tree parking area.

Near Grant Grove

Azalea Trail ★ This is a pleasant trail at any time, and particularly beautiful in late June and early July when the azaleas along Sequoia Creek are in full, fragrant bloom. From the visitor center, walk past the amphitheater to the Sunset Campground and cross CA 180. The first mile joins the South Boundary Trail as it meanders through Wilsonia and criss-crosses Sequoia Creek in a gentle climb. After 1.5 miles, you'll come to the third crossing of Sequoia Creek, which may be dry in late summer but still lush with ferns and brightly colored azaleas along its banks. Return the way you came.

3 miles/1–2 hr. Easy. The trail head begins at the Kings Canyon Visitor Center.

Day Hikes & Scenic Walks

Big Stump Trail ★ You'll see the results of logging at its worst on this trail that meanders through what was once a grove of giant sequoias. All that's left today are the old stumps and piles of 100-year-old sawdust. A brochure available at the visitor centers describes the logging that occurred here in the 1880s. To continue onward, see the Hitchcock Meadow Trail described below, which leads to Viola Fall.

1 mile/1 hr. Easy. Begin at the Big Stump Picnic Area near the CA 180 entrance to Grant Grove from Kings Canyon.

Dead Giant Loop ★ This easy, meandering loop trail takes you along a lush meadow to the shell of what was once an impressive forest giant. The Dead Giant Loop and the North Grove Loop (described below) share the first 0.8 miles. The trail descends a fire road and, after 0.3 miles, hits a junction. Take the lower trail, continuing along the fire road. After another 0.5 miles, you'll break off from the North Grove Loop and head south around a lush meadow. It's another 0.3 miles to a sign that reads DEAD GIANT. Turn right (west) to see what's left of this large sequoia. The trail climbs slightly as it circles a knoll and comes to Sequoia Lake Overlook. The lake was formed in 1899 when the Kings River Lumber Company built a dam on Mill Flat Creek. The water was diverted down a flume to the town of Sanger. During the logging era, millions of board feet of giant sequoias were floated down that flume to be finished at a mill in Sanger. Continue around the loop back to the DEAD GIANT sign and then head back to the parking area.

2.3 miles/1½ hr. Easy. The trail head is at the lower end of the General Grant Tree parking area. It begins near a locked gate with a sign that reads NORTH GROVE LOOP.

General Grant Tree Trail ★★ This walk leads to the huge General Grant Tree, which is the nation's only living national shrine. In 1956, President Eisenhower gave the Grant Tree this designation in memory of Americans who gave their lives in wartime. The walk includes signs to help visitors interpret forest features.

0.5 miles/30 min. Easy. Begin at the Grant Tree parking area 1 mile northwest of the visitor center.

Hitchcock Meadow Trail ★ See pretty Viola Fall on this hike that winds among trees logged more than 100 years ago. The first 0.5 miles is on the Big Stump Trail described

Hikes near Grant Grove

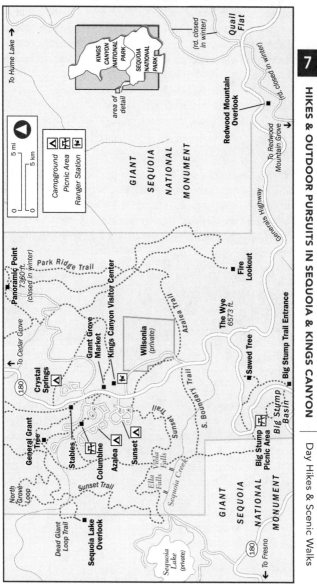

above; continue hiking another 0.3 miles to the Hitchcock sequoia stumps. Notice the small sequoias in this area; they are descendants of the giant sequoias logged in the last century. At this point, the trail climbs slightly to a ridge, where it reenters Kings Canyon National Park before descending steeply to Sequoia Creek. Cross the creek on a culvert bridge toward a sign directing hikers to Viola Fall, a series of short steps that, during high water, merge into a single waterfall. It's dangerous to venture down into the canyon, but above it are several flat places that make great picnic spots.

3.5 miles/2 hr. Easy. Begin at the Big Stump Picnic Area near the entrance to Grant Grove from Kings Canyon.

North Grove Loop ★   Lightly traveled trail follows an abandoned mill road from yesteryear. It cuts through stands of dogwood, sugar pine, sequoia, and white fir. You'll find a large, dead sequoia that shows evidence of a fire.

1.5 miles/1–2 hr. Easy. Begin at the lower end of the General Grant Tree parking area.

Park Ridge Trail ★★   On a clear day, you'll be able to see the coastal mountains 100 miles away on this ridgetop trail. Begin by walking south along the ridge, where views of the valley and peaks dominate. You'll be able to see Hume Lake in Sequoia National Forest, the San Joaquin Valley, and occasionally the Coast Range. Return the way you came.

4.7 miles/3 hr. Easy. Begin at the Panoramic Point parking area, a 2.5-mile drive down a steep road from Grant Grove Village.

Sunset Trail ★   This hike climbs 1,400 feet past two waterfalls and a lake. After crossing the highway, the trail moves to the left around a campground. After 1.3 miles, you'll follow the South Boundary Trail toward Viola Fall. You'll then reach a paved road where you can head to the right to see the park's original entrance. Return the way you came, or follow the road to the General Grant Tree parking area and walk to the visitor center.

6 miles/3–4 hr. Moderate to strenuous. Begin across the road from the Kings Canyon Visitor Center.

Near Cedar Grove

Bubbs Creek Trail ★   This strenuous hike provides beautiful canyon and waterfall views. Begin by crossing and recrossing Copper Creek. This site was once an American Indian village, and shards of obsidian can still be found on the ground. After the first mile, you'll enter a swampy area that offers a good place to watch for wildlife. The trail here closes in on the river, where deer and bears drink. At 2 miles, you'll come to a junction. The trail to Paradise Valley heads north (left), while the hike to Bubbs Creek veers right and crosses Bailey Bridge, over the South Fork of the Kings River. Continue east over the four small wooden bridges that cross Bubbs Creek. The creek was named after John Bubbs, a prospector and rancher who arrived here in 1864. The trail will climb on the creek's north side, throwing in a few steep switchbacks to keep you alert. The switchbacks provide nice views of the canyon of Paradise Valley and Cedar Grove.

At 3 miles, you'll come to a large emerald pool with waterfalls. Far above is a rock formation known as the Sphinx—John Muir named the feature after Egypt's famous likeness. At 4 miles, you'll reach Sphinx Creek, a nice place to spend the day or night (with a wilderness permit). There are several campsites nearby. Hike back the way you came or on the Sentinel Trail.

8 miles/5 hr. Moderate to strenuous. The trail head is at the east end of the parking area at Road's End.

Mist Falls ★★ This is one of the more popular trails leading to the backcountry, but it also makes a nice day hike. The first 2 miles are dry, until you reach Bubbs Creek Bridge. Take the fork to the left and head uphill. The first waterfall is a pretty spot to take a break. From here, the trail meanders along the river, and through forest and swamp areas, before it comes out at the base of Mist Falls, a wide expanse of a waterfall that flows generously in spring. There are dozens of great picnic spots here and along the way up. Return along the same route or, at Bubbs Creek Bridge, cross over and head back on the Sentinel Trail, which adds a mile to the hike. From Mist Falls, you can also continue to Paradise Valley, described below.

8 miles/2–3 hr. Moderate to strenuous. Begin at the short-term parking area at Road's End past Cedar Grove Village and follow the signs.

Muir's Rock ★ Okay, so you can't walk too far, don't have time, etc. Well, now there's no excuse. This level, simple, short stroll takes you to one of the most historically significant spots in the park's modern-day history. From this wide, flat rock, John Muir delivered impassioned speeches about the Sierra. When referring to logging the giant trees, he said that mankind may as well "sell the rain clouds and the snow and the rivers to be cut up and carried away, if that were possible."

300 ft./10 min. Easy. The pulpit is 300 ft. from the parking area at Road's End, along the trail to Zumwalt Meadow.

Paradise Valley ★★ This makes a great overnight hike—the valley is pretty and there's much to explore—but it can also be accomplished as an ambitious day hike. Follow the Mist Falls trail to the falls and then head up 3 miles of switchbacks to Paradise Valley. The valley is 3 miles long, relatively flat, and beautiful. Hike through the valley to connect with the John Muir Trail and the rest of the backcountry, or return the way you came.

12 miles/7–10 hr. Moderate to strenuous. Begin at the short-term parking area at Road's End past Cedar Grove Village and follow the signs.

River Trail ★ River views and a powerful waterfall add interest to this trail, which heads upstream as it hugs the river. You can shorten it if you want by just walking to the falls (0.5 miles round-trip) or Zumwalt Meadow (3 miles round-trip; a shorter version is listed below). The waterfalls are 0.3 miles along the trail. The falls are short but powerful—do *not* attempt to climb them. Just north of the falls, back toward the parking area, is a sign that reads ZUMWALT MEADOW—ROAD'S END. Take this trail, which initially hugs the highway before breaking off into a beautiful canyon. At 1.5 miles is the Zumwalt Bridge. If you were to cross the bridge, you'd be 0.3 miles from the Zumwalt Meadow parking area. Do not cross the bridge; instead, continue onward up the canyon for another 0.3 miles to Zumwalt Meadow. From here there's a slight incline. In 0.5 miles you'll reach a fork; keep right. The rest of the hike follows the riverbank, which sports plenty of swimming and fishing holes. After 2.5 miles, you'll come to another footbridge. Cross over and it's a short 0.5-mile walk back to the Road's End parking area, where you can try to catch a ride. Otherwise, retrace your steps back to your car.

5.5 miles/4 hr. Easy. From the Cedar Grove Ranger Station, drive 3.1 miles to the Roaring River Falls parking area.

Zumwalt Meadow ★   This hike takes you across a lovely meadow, with lots of broad views. Cross the bridge and walk left for 300 feet to a fork. Take the trail that leads to the right for a bird's-eye view of the meadow below before descending 50 feet. The trail runs along the meadow's edge, where the fragrance of ponderosa pine, sugar pine, and incense cedar fill the air. The loop returns along the banks of the South Fork of the Kings River; watch for Grand Sentinel and North Dome rising in the background.

1.5 miles/1 hr. Easy. The trail begins at the Zumwalt Meadow parking area, 1 mile west of Road's End, past Cedar Grove Village.

Elsewhere in the Parks

Cold Springs Nature Trail (in Sequoia's Mineral King) ★

This easy loop showcases the natural history and beauty of the region. It passes near private cabins left over from the days before 1978, when the Mineral King area was added to Sequoia National Park. The walk offers views of the Mineral King Valley and surrounding peaks. It can get hot and dry in summer, so carry additional water.

2 miles/1 hr. Easy. Begin at Mineral King's Cold Springs Campground, across from the ranger station.

Kings River National Recreation Trail ★★

It's a long drive to the trail head, but after a hike in upper Kings Canyon, this is a great place to see what the canyon looks like from the bottom. The views here rival anything in the park, with peaks towering overhead and the river rushing nearby. The first mile alternates between rapids and pools that offer great fishing. At 1.5 miles, you can see up Converse Creek and its rugged canyon. At 3 miles, you'll find Spring Creek, a short but pretty waterfall and a good place to rest. You can turn around here for a total hike of 6 miles or proceed for the 10-mile option.

From this point, the trail ascends the steep Garlic Spur, a ridge that ends suddenly at the ledge of the canyon. The trail above Spring Creek is flecked with obsidian, the nearest source of which is the Mono Craters, more than 100 miles to the north. For that reason, many believe this trail was used for trading by the Monache Indians. After the long, steep ascent, the trail heads down to Garlic Meadow Creek. A short distance upstream are large pools and wide resting areas. Beyond the creek, the trail is not maintained.

6–10 miles/4–8 hr., depending on distance traveled. Easy to Spring Creek; strenuous to Garlic Meadow Creek. On CA 180, 6 miles west of Big Stump Entrance, turn north on FS Rd. 12SO1, a dirt road marked MCKENZIE HELIPORT, DELILAH LOOKOUT, CAMP 4.5 MILES. Drive 18 miles to the Kings River. Turn west and drive 2½ miles to Rodgers Crossing. Cross the bridge and turn east, following signs to the Kings River Trail. The trail head is at the east end of a parking lot another 7 miles ahead, at the road's end.

Marble Fork Trail (in Sequoia's Foothills) ★★

This is one of the most scenic hikes in the Foothills area of Sequoia National Park. The walk leads to a deep gorge, where the roaring Marble Fall spills in a cascade over multi-colored boulders. From the parking area, begin hiking north up the Southern California Edison flume. After crossing the flume on a wooden bridge, watch on the right for a trail sign and head east uphill. The trail has some steep switchbacks and is near some large poison oak bushes that sport stems 3 inches wide. Watch out for these bare sticks in late fall and winter.

The trail then begins to flatten out and settle into a slight slope for the rest of the hike up to the waterfalls. Look for large yuccas and California bay trees along the way. After 2 miles, you'll be able to see the waterfalls as the trail cuts through white-and-gray marble. Once you reach the falls, it's almost impossible to hike any farther, so don't attempt it. The marble slabs break easily, and boulders in the area can get slick. Be extra careful when the water is high. This is a good hike year-round but can be hot during summer. Upon your return, be sure to check yourself thoroughly for ticks.

6 miles/4–6 hr. Strenuous. Follow the dirt road at the upper end of Potwisha Campground, which is 3¾ miles east of the Ash Mountain Entrance. There is a small parking area past campsite no. 16.

Potwisha and River's Edge ★

At one time, an American Indian village known as Potwisha thrived here, home to a tribe of Monache. The main village was just about where the dump station is now. On the bedrock are mortar holes where the women ground acorns into meal. From here, the trail continues up the river to a sandy beach and a good swimming hole. The trail turns east upstream before the suspension bridge, then northward up a short but steep hill to the road. Turn west (left) and hike the short distance back to the parking area.

0.5 miles/30 min. Easy. From the Ash Mountain Entrance, take the highway to the Potwisha Campground. At the campground entrance (which will be to your left), turn right down a paved road toward an RV dump station until it hits a dead end at a parking area. Continue toward the river on a footpath to open bedrock.

Wildman Meadow (Sequoia National Forest) ★★

This hike through the Monarch Wilderness starts with a relatively easy trek to Deer Cove. After reaching Deer Cove, it's a steep ascent to 7,500 feet—a 1,900-foot gain in 5 miles. From Deer Cove, hike 3.5 miles to a sandy knoll and a good view into the rugged canyon drainage area of Grizzly Creek. At 6.5 miles, you'll top the ridge and cross over to the north-facing slope. A quick drop lands you in Wildman Meadow.

14 miles/10 hr. Strenuous. The trail head for Deer Cove Trail is just north of CA 180, 2½ miles west of Cedar Grove and the Kings Canyon border in the Sequoia National Forest.

EXPLORING THE BACKCOUNTRY

Finding quiet and solitude is not nearly as difficult here as it is in Yosemite. Mineral King and the Giant Forest in Sequoia, along with Cedar Grove in Kings Canyon, are the main points of entry into the backcountry, but the wilderness here is never farther than 5 miles in any direction. It surrounds the park, and just about any hike that lasts more than an hour will get you into the wild.

Mineral King, in Sequoia, is a quiet spot that attracts few people to its 11 trails because the road to the glacial valley is so difficult to drive. Avalanches have swept swaths of trees aside, and the valley floor is covered with wild meadows. Higher up, there are woods of red fir, white fir, and lodgepole pine. The landscape is rocky but colorful. Alpine trails begin at 7,500 feet and climb from there.

Cedar Grove, in Kings Canyon, is at the dead end of CA 180. From here, to the north and east, the park is inaccessible to vehicular traffic. Hikes from Cedar Grove head out toward the Rae Lakes Loop, Monarch Wilderness, and beyond.

Preparing for Backcountry Trips

Be sure to get a detailed topographical map before setting off on any overnight hike. Maps are available at all ranger stations and at visitor centers throughout the park. You may want to pick up a copy of a free trip-planning guide for the wilderness areas of the parks, available at park visitor centers or by calling the **wilderness office** at ✆ **559/565-3766** to request one.

PERMITS & FEES All overnight backpacking stays in Sequoia & Kings Canyon require a wilderness permit, available at www.nps.gov/seki/planyourvisit/wilderness_permits. htm through a downloaded application. Permits cost $10 plus $5 per person. Outside the quota season, which is generally May to September, they are free and can be obtained from drop boxes located outside visitor centers/permit stations.

Reservations can be made at least 14 days in advance, from March 1 to mid-September. To reserve a permit, you must provide a name, address, telephone number, the number of people in your party, the number of stock if applicable, start and end dates, start and end trail heads, a principal destination, and a rough itinerary. Download the application from the park's website and email it, or mail it to **Wilderness Permit Reservations,** Sequoia & Kings Canyon National Parks, 47050 Generals Hwy. #60, Three Rivers, CA 93271. Reserved permits must be picked up by 9am of the date of entry. If you're delayed, call the ranger station or else you risk forfeiting your permit. If your hike crosses agency boundaries, get the permit from the agency on whose land the hike begins. Only one permit is required.

For hikes beginning in Sequoia National Forest (or in Giant Sequoia National Monument, which is managed as a section of this national forest) permits are not required, with one exception: Golden Trout Wilderness is the only wilderness in the Sequoia National Forest that requires a permit for overnight stays. Permits are not required for day use in any wilderness within Sequoia National Forest. For further information, call ✆ **559/784-1500,** or visit www.fs.fed.us/r5/sequoia. In the Sierra National Forest, permits are also free. For maps and further information, contact the **Sierra National Forest** (www.fs.fed.us/r5/sierra; ✆ **559/297-0706**).

Exploring the Backcountry

HIKES & OUTDOOR PURSUITS IN SEQUOIA & KINGS CANYON

The Inyo National Forest administers areas that stretch from the Sierra Crest to Owens Valley. Most trails here have quotas, and free permits are required. Reservations are available 3 months in advance and cost $5 per person, or $15 for Mount Whitney, which are issued through a lottery. For reservations, contact **Wilderness Permit Reservations,** Inyo National Forest (www.fs.fed.us/r5/inyo; ✆ **760/873-2400**).

Inyo National Forest extends 165 miles near the California and Nevada border, covering about 2 million acres. Like all national forests, the Inyo is managed for both ecosystem health and multiple uses. In addition to recreation, the Inyo National Forest is also used for timber, minerals, watershed, and providing fish and wildlife habitat.

Recreational opportunities include camping, picnicking, hiking, fishing, equestrian use, as well as off-highway vehicle use. Ski resorts offer alpine skiing and snowboarding, with over 100 miles of trails groomed for multiple purpose winter use (snowmobile, ski, and snowshoe) and approximately 45 miles of trails groomed for cross-country skiing.

Inyo National Forest is divided into four Ranger Districts: Mono Lake, Mammoth, White Mountain, and Mt. Whitney. Each district has a Ranger Station and/or Visitor Center. For general information see www.fs.fed.us/r5/inyo or call ✆ **760/ 873-2400.**

SPECIAL REGULATIONS & WARNINGS   Be aware of bears that frequent these regions. Stay off high peaks during thunderstorms, and don't attempt any climb if it looks as though a storm is rolling in; exposed peaks are often struck by lightning. In the summer months, mosquitoes and sunburn are real problems, so bring plenty of repellent and sunscreen. As always, come prepared for temperature changes. At higher elevations, even in the middle of summer, cold weather can be hazardous.

Overnight Hikes

There are 14 ranger stations in the wilderness of the park. Eight are along the John Muir and Pacific Crest trails. Another six are in the southern part of the park in the Sequoia backcountry. Most are not staffed fall through spring. *Note:* Many of the following routes are buried under snow in winter.

Exploring the Backcountry

High Sierra Trail ★★   Head for the backcountry on this popular route that some people use as a one-way passage to Mount Whitney. The trail gets a lot of sun, so begin early in the day. From the parking area, head out on a paved trail to the south (straight), cross several bridges, and arrive at a junction. Turn right onto the High Sierra Trail. You will pass Eagle View, the Wolverton Cutoff, and Panther Creek. Hike at least 3 miles before setting up camp. For $360 double (meals included; $75 for one additional person), the "civilized" lodging option is the 11-mile hike from Crescent Meadow to the **Bearpaw High Sierra Camp** (www.visit sequoia.com; ☏ **866/575-4211**).

At least 10 miles/5 hr. Strenuous. Take CA 198 to Giant Forest and proceed to Crescent Meadow Rd. Bear right at the junction, passing the signed parking area for Moro Rock. The road ends at the Crescent Meadow parking area.

Jennie Lakes Trail ★   Spend time at beautiful Jennie Lake on this nice overnight hike that's not too demanding and can be extended into the Jennie Lakes Wilderness Area. From the parking area, cross through the campground and cross Big Meadow Creek. The trail climbs from here. At Fox Meadow, there is a wooden trail sign and a register for hikers to sign. At the next junction, head right toward Jennie Lake (left goes toward the Weaver Lake Trail) and up to Poop Out Pass. From here, it's a drop down to the Boulder Creek drainage area and on to emerald-green Jennie Lake. This hike can be combined with a second day hike to Weaver Lake: Just retrace your steps to the Weaver Lake turnoff. Weaver Lake is a relatively warm mountain lake surrounded by blueberry bushes that reportedly are heavy with fresh fruit in July. Camp at least a quarter-mile from the lakeshore.

At least 12 miles/7 hr. Moderate to strenuous. From Grant Grove, drive about 7 miles south on the Generals Hwy. to the turnoff for Big Meadows Campground. The trail head and parking are on the south side of the road next to a ranger station.

Lakes Trail ★★   This trail moves along a string of tarns— high mountain lakes created by the scouring action of glaciers thousands of years ago. Heather Lake and Pear Lake are popular destinations along this route. From the trail head, go straight ahead (east), avoiding the Long Meadow Trail.

Climb up a moraine ridge and soon you'll be hiking above Wolverton Creek, which darts through small meadows strewn with wildflowers. At a junction with the Panther Gap Trail, head left toward Heather Lake. At a second junction, you'll have to choose your direction. To the right is Hump Trail, a steep but always open trail, with no extreme drop-offs. To the left is Watchtower Trail, which moves along a granite ledge blasted in the rock with dynamite. With the Tokopah Valley far below, the Watchtower Trail hike is not for those who suffer vertigo. Both trails wind up at Heather Lake. Camping is not allowed here but is okay farther up the trail at Pear and Emerald lakes.

At least 13 miles/7 hr. Moderate to strenuous. From Giant Forest, drive north on the Generals Hwy. to the Wolverton parking area. The trail head is on the left of the parking lot as you enter from the highway.

OTHER SPORTS & ACTIVITIES

CROSS-COUNTRY SKIING   There are 35 miles of marked backcountry trails in the parks. For information, call park concessionaires (© **559/335-5500** in Grant Grove, **559/565-4070** in the Wuksachi Lodge area).

In Sequoia, the **Pear Lake Winter Hut** is open to the public for overnight backcountry accommodations from mid-December through April for $50 per person per night. The hut is equipped with a pellet stove and cooking gear, but guests need to bring their own food. The hike is almost 7 miles one-way and has a 3,000-foot gain. Reservations are by a November lottery, but there are often openings during the season. Call © **559/565-4251** for more information.

FISHING   Open all year for trout fishing—rainbow, brook, German brown, and golden trout—are the Kaweah drainage, the parks' lakes, and a section of the South Fork of the Kings River. Most other waters are open for trout fishing from late April to mid-November, and for other species year-round. California fishing licenses (available at stores in the park) are required for anglers 16 and older; you should also get a copy of the National Park Service's fishing regulations, available at visitor centers.

HORSEBACK RIDING   Guided horseback and mule rides and overnight pack trips are offered by concessionaires in both parks and the adjacent national monument during the summer. In Kings Canyon, **Cedar Grove Pack Station** (© **559/565-3464** in summer, 559/337-2413 in winter) is located about 1 mile east of Cedar Grove Village, and **Grant Grove Stables** (© **559/335-9292**) is located near Grant Grove Village. In Giant Sequoia National Monument, **Big Meadow** (© **559/565-3404** in summer, 559/667-8499 in winter) is located on Big Meadows Road, 10 miles east of Generals Highway. The pack stations offer hourly rides as well as overnight treks, while the stables offer day rides only. Rates are $40 for a 1-hour ride and $75 for a 2-hour trip; call for current charges for pack trips.

SNOWSHOEING   Free ranger-led snowshoe tours take place in both parks on Saturdays and holidays when conditions permit. Call © **559/565-4480** (Wuksachi) or © **559/565-4307** (Grant Grove). There are also several snowshoe trails around **Wuksachi Lodge** (© **559/565-070**); rentals are available at the lodge.

WHITE-WATER BOATING   The Kaweah and Upper Kings rivers within the parks are not open to boating (neither kayaks nor inflatable rafts), but several companies run trips on the rivers just outside the parks. You're guaranteed to get wet on this thrilling roller-coaster ride through the rapids; it's a great way not only to see these scenic rivers, but also to experience them close up.

   Whitewater Voyages (www.whitewatervoyages.com; © **800/400-7238**) offers trips on the Kings and Kern rivers, with rates that range from $99 to $219 for half- and full-day trips. Multiday trips are also available (call for rates). **Kings River Expeditions** (www.kingsriver.com; © **800/846-3674** or 559/233-4881) specializes in rafting trips on the Kings River. Day trips run $85 (student special) to $165 per person. Overnight trips are also available (call for rates).

Other Sports & Activities

HIKES & OUTDOOR PURSUITS IN SEQUOIA & KINGS CANYON

WHERE TO STAY & EAT IN SEQUOIA & KINGS CANYON

Welcome to the land of the giants. Five lodges and 14 campgrounds are scattered throughout Sequoia & Kings Canyon National Parks, with others in nearby Giant Sequoia National Monument. Though the colossal trees are these parks' main attractions, flower-filled meadows, serene lakes, and stunning backcountry views can also be found here. Those who prefer comfortable hotels will find a variety of options, both within and outside the parks, ranging from inexpensive mom-and-pop motels to historic bed-and-breakfast inns and delightful mountain lodges. Campers should have little trouble finding a spot to pitch a tent or park an RV. However, be aware that no RV hookups are available in the parks or monument. As for food, there are a variety of interesting choices.

The three primary gateway communities discussed in this chapter are all along CA 198. **Visalia,** centered on a charming downtown, is 36 miles from Sequoia National Park's Ash Mountain Entrance and the largest city in the area, with the most facilities. Closer to the parks are **Lemon Cove,** 11 miles from the park border, and **Three Rivers,** 7 miles from the park border.

Note: From several miles inside the Ash Mountain Entrance to Giant Forest, the Generals Highway is narrow and winding and not recommended for vehicles more than 22 feet long; these should enter the parks from CA 180.

LODGING

Inside the Parks

MODERATE

Silver City Mountain Resort ★ If you're heading for the remote Mineral King area, this is your only lodging option. But, this historic cabin resort is an excellent choice for those seeking a woodsy experience off the beaten track. There are three types of cabins here, with a variety of bed combinations (some sleep up to eight) and woodstoves for heat. The top-of-the-line Swiss Chalets are finished in knotty pine with completely equipped kitchens, full bathrooms, and outdoor barbecues. The midlevel units, dubbed Family Cabins, have two bedrooms and complete kitchens, propane wall lamps, plus electric lights, small restrooms with toilets but no showers (there is a central bathhouse), and decks with barbecue grills. Historical Cabins, built in the 1930s, are the most basic units, with light from propane lamps, plus a camp kitchen. Most have refrigerators, and all share the bathhouse.

Mineral King, Sequoia National Park, CA 93262. www.silvercity resort.com. ℰ **559/242-3510.** 13 cabins (6 w/shared central bathhouse), 3 hotel rooms. $165–$525. 2–3 night minimum stay. Located 21 miles up Mineral King Rd. Closed late Oct to Memorial Day. **Amenities:** Restaurant (see p. 140); limited Wi-Fi in common areas.

Wuksachi Lodge ★★ The Wuksachi Lodge is the newest and the most upscale lodging in Sequoia & Kings Canyon. Rooms are in three buildings separated from the lodge by parking lots. Views out the windows are dominated by the forest and surrounding mountains. The standard units have two queen-size beds and a small desk; deluxe rooms are larger, with two queen-size beds or a king-size and a sofa bed, plus a table and two chairs; what are called superior rooms are actually mini-suites, with two queen-size beds or one king, plus a sofa bed in an alcove sitting area with a sliding door (a good place for your teenager). Another plus: A trail starting here winds 3.1 miles through the forest to Lodgepole or extend your hike by meeting up with the Twin Lakes Trail for an 11-mile hike.

CA 180 and CA 198, Sequoia National Park, CA 93262. www.visit sequoia.com. ℰ **866/908-0804** or 559/625-7700. 102 units. May–Oct and holidays $226–$335; Nov–Apr $133–$184. **Amenities:** Restaurant (see **Peaks Restaurant,** p. 139); lounge; free Wi-Fi.

INEXPENSIVE

Cedar Grove Lodge ★   Location, location, location. This motel is basic but set on the bank of the Kings River. It's a 36-mile drive down a winding highway that provides beautiful vistas along the way. The rooms are standard motel units—clean and comfortable, but nothing special. But you're surrounded by tall trees with a pretty river running by. Most of the units are above the snack bar and boast communal decks with river views. But the three smaller rooms on ground level are the prize, because they offer private patios looking right out on the river.

CA 180 (P.O. Box 907), Cedar Grove, Kings Canyon National Park, CA 93633. www.visitsequoia.com. © **866/908-0804** or 559/565-3096. 18 units. $151–$200 double. Closed Nov–Apr. **Amenities:** Restaurant (see "Where to Eat," p. 139).

Grant Grove Cabins ★   Although all accommodations here are cabins, there's a wide range of amenities and prices to be found, from handsomely restored units that have historical ambience to rustic tent-cabins that simply provide a comfortable bed out of the weather at a very low cost. Those who want to rough it in style should reserve one of the nine cabins built in the 1920s; these have electricity, indoor plumbing, and private bathrooms. A bit less modern, but still quite comfortable, are the 43 rustic cabins that have kerosene lanterns for light and a shared bathhouse. Some are wooden cabins; others, available in summer only, have wood floors and walls but canvas roofs. All units have full linen service. It's a 10-minute walk from the cabins to the Kings Canyon Visitor Center in Grant Grove; nearby is the **Grant Grove Restaurant** (see p. 139).

CA 180 (P.O. Box 907), Grant Grove Village, Kings Canyon National Park, CA 93633. www.visitsequoia.com. © **866/908-0804** or 559/335-5500. 53 units (9 w/private bathroom), $89–$259. Lower prices in winter. Register at John Muir Lodge. **Amenities:** Restaurant.

John Muir Lodge ★★   This handsome log lodge, built in 1998, looks perfect in its beautiful national park setting. A mountain-lodge atmosphere prevails here. It's an excellent choice for visitors who want quiet, comfortable, modern accommodations, with full bathrooms and coffeemakers, situated in a forest environment. Standard rooms offer two queen-size beds and wonderful views of the surrounding woods. Suites consist of two connecting standard rooms, except that one of the rooms has a queen-size bed and a queen sofa sleeper instead of two queens.

CA 180 (P.O. Box 907), Grant Grove Village, Kings Canyon National Park, CA 93633. www.visitsequoia.com. *©* **866/908-0804** or 559/335-5500. 86 units. $90–$245 double. Register at John Muir Lodge in Grant Grove Village. **Amenities:** Limited free Wi-Fi in common areas.

Outside the Parks
IN GIANT SEQUOIA NATIONAL MONUMENT
Moderate

Montecito Sequoia Lodge ★   If you're looking for a family-style holiday, this may be your place. The Montecito caters to families and large groups, with recreation of all types—from fishing and fencing to cross-country skiing (85 miles of groomed trails begin here). There's even a small lake, offering seasonal sailing and canoeing. Recreation is more limited in winter, when options include snowshoeing and ice skating. The guest rooms, all of which have private bathrooms, are in four separate buildings; 13 cabins share two bathhouses. Bed types and numbers vary, with units that sleep from two to eight. Meals are included in the price and served buffet style.

8000 Generals Hwy., Giant Sequoia National Monument, Kings Canyon National Park, CA 93633. www.mslodge.com. *©* **800/227-9900,** or 559/565-3388. 36 units, plus 13 cabins w/2 shared bathhouses. $115–$459 double. 6-night (Sun–Fri) minimum stay in summer except Sat, when 1-night stays are allowed. Rates include all meals. Take CA 180 into Kings Canyon National Park, turn right at the fork, and drive 8 miles south to the lodge entrance, turn right, and follow the road about ½ mile to the parking lot. **Amenities:** Dining room; bar; children's and teen programs; Jacuzzi; large heated outdoor pool; 2 outdoor tennis courts; watersports equipment; free Wi-Fi (limited signal).

Stony Creek Lodge ★   This small, basic inn, sister property to Montecito Sequoia Lodge, offers motel-style accommodations in a pretty setting in Giant Sequoia National Monument, about 20 minutes south of Grant Grove. The guest rooms are basic but pleasant and sleep from two to four, and there's usually a fire blazing in the lobby fireplace. There's also a pizzeria, laundromat, showers ($5), and gas station here. Breakfast is included in the tariff.

Generals Hwy., Giant Sequoia National Monument, Kings Canyon National Park, CA 93633. www.mslodge.com/stonycreeklodge.

ⓒ **800/227-9900** or 559/565-3909. 12 units. $219–$299 double; breakfast included. Closed Oct–May. Take the Stony Creek Village exit off the Generals Hwy., between Grant Grove Village and Wuksachi. **Amenities:** Restaurant (seasonal, sporadic hours); store; TV; free Wi-Fi.

IN THE NEARBY GATEWAY TOWNS

In addition to the properties discussed below, reliable chains in Visalia include the **Holiday Inn Express,** 5625 W. Cypress Ave. (ⓒ **559/627-0600**), which has rates of $89 to $139 double; and the **La Quinta Inn & Suites,** 5438 W. Cypress Ave. (ⓒ **559/235-5100**), charging $119 to $129 double. A solid independent motel, the **Lamp Liter Inn,** 3300 W. Mineral King Ave. (www.lampliter.net; ⓒ **800/662-6692** or 559/732-4511), features cabin suites set off from a nice pool courtyard for $189 and double rooms for $72 to $125. Lodging options in Three Rivers include the **Western Holiday Lodge,** 40105 Sierra Dr. (ⓒ **559/561-4119**), which charges $130 to $160 double; and the **Comfort Inn & Suites,** 40820 Sierra Dr. (ⓒ **800/331-2140** or 559/561-9000), charging $162 to $196 double. All have lower rates in the winter.

Moderate

Buckeye Tree Lodge ★★   Watch the river roll by from your patio or balcony at this lodge that's just a quarter of a mile from the entrance to Sequoia National Park. The Buckeye Tree offers affordable and attractive rooms, not to mention rolling lawns that end at a picturesque river. Every unit has a patio or balcony offering splendid views of the main fork of the Kaweah River. Accommodations are clean, basic motel units. Eight units have showers only; the rest have tub/showers.

46000 Sierra Dr., Three Rivers, CA 93271. www.buckeyetreelodge.com. ⓒ **559/561-5900.** 12 units. $129–$219 double. Lower winter rates. Rates include breakfast basket. Pets accepted ($15/night). **Amenities:** Outdoor pool; DVD library; free Wi-Fi.

Lazy J Ranch Motel ★   This popular motel offers great mountain and river views, plus cozy rooms, some with gas fireplaces. Owned by the Johnson family since the 1970s, the Lazy J is on 10 acres in the foothills near Sequoia National Park and has a spacious countryside setting with pastures, as well as a well-groomed lawn and pool area. Recreational activities include fishing, sailing, boating, waterskiing, and swimming in nearby Lake Kaweah.

39625 Sierra Dr., Three Rivers, CA 93271. www.lazyjranchmotel.com. © 559/561-4449. 18 units, $160–$225; breakfast included. Lower rates in winter. Pets accepted ($10 charge per pet). **Amenities:** Outdoor pool; free Wi-Fi.

Plantation Bed & Breakfast ★ Salute America's national park system at Plantation B&B. The 7-unit inn, which formerly had a Southern Belle theme, now lauds Sequoia, Kings Canyon, Yosemite, the Grand Canyon, and other national parks. One thing that didn't change was the honeymoon suite, which is still decorated in an elegant bordello style, with a king-size bed and an enormous mirror, a red crystal chandelier, and a clawfoot bathtub painted with a tasteful nude. Two rooms have showers only, while the others have showers and tubs. Secluded in a palm-shaded area surrounded by orange groves are a large swimming pool and a Jacuzzi. The wonderful breakfasts include fresh fruit, homemade granola, and a hot entree such as crème brûlée French toast.

33038 CA 198, Lemon Cove, CA 93244. www.theplantation.net. © 559/597-2555. 7 units. $145–$209 double. Rates include breakfast. Located on CA 198, 16 miles west of the park entrance. **Amenities:** Large pool; Jacuzzi; free Wi-Fi.

Rio Sierra Riverhouse ★ Pull up a beach chair. This riverfront inn offers something special for guests who visit on a hot summer day: a place to wade, sit on a rock or hunker down in a beach chair as the river rolls by. Rio Sierra Riverhouse, six miles from the entrance to Sequoia National Park, is in the middle of Three Rivers. Guests laud it because the staff is friendly and they enjoy hearing the sounds of the river at night.

41997 Sierra Dr., Three Rivers, CA 93271. www.rio-sierra.com. © 559/561-4720. 4 units. $225–$325. Lower winter rates. **Amenities:** Free Wi-Fi.

Sequoia Village Inn ★★ The sister property of the Buckeye Tree Lodge (p. 131) across the street, the Sequoia Village Inn offers charming cabin-style units that sleep two to eight. Stylishly decorated with lodgepole bed frames and hardwood floors, they're great for couples and families alike.

Many feature full kitchens and decks with great views; the smaller units have microwaves and fridges only.

43175 Sierra Dr., Three Rivers, CA 93271. www.sequoiavillageinn.com. ℭ **559/561-3652.** 10 units. $139–$449. Lower winter rates. **Amenities:** Outdoor pool, barbecues; movie library; free Wi-Fi.

Visalia Marriott at the Convention Center ★★

The best hotel in Visalia—located a block off bustling Main Street—offers reliable Marriott service and style in its rooms and facilities. The rooms are chic and comfortable; units on the eighth floor feature private balconies and great city views.

300 S. Court St., Visalia, CA 93291. www.marriott.com. ℭ **559/636-1111.** 197 units, including 5 suites. $150–$200 double; $200–$280 suite. Pets accepted ($75 fee). **Amenities:** Restaurant (steakhouse); bar; exercise room; outdoor pool; free Wi-Fi.

CAMPING

There are numerous camping opportunities both within and surrounding Sequoia & Kings Canyon National Parks. Brief descriptions of individual campgrounds follow, and you'll find additional details in the campground chart on p. 134.

It's important to remember that, when camping in this area, proper food storage is *required* for the sake of the black bears in the parks as well as your safety. See local bulletin boards for instructions.

Note: You'll need a wilderness permit to stay overnight in the backcountry; see "Exploring the Backcountry" on p. 121.

In Sequoia National Park

Campgrounds in the national park that accept reservations are accessible by phone and website at (www.recreation.gov; ℭ **877/444-6777**). Reservations for some park campgrounds are taken up to 6 months in advance; some other campgrounds are on a first-come, first-served basis. Additional information on the national park campgrounds (but not reservations) can be obtained by calling the general Sequoia & Kings Canyon information line at ℭ **559/565-3341.**

The two biggest campgrounds in the park are in the Lodgepole area. The **Lodgepole Campground ★**, which has vault toilets, is often crowded, but it's pretty and not far from some spectacular big trees. Nearby backcountry trails offer some solitude. Close to the campground are a grocery store,

Sequoia & Kings Canyon Campgrounds

CAMPGROUND	ELEV. (FT.)	TOTAL SITES	RV HOOKUPS	DUMP STATION
INSIDE SEQUOIA NATIONAL PARK				
Atwell Mill	6,650	21	0	No
Buckeye Flat	2,800	28	0	No
Cold Springs	7,500	31	0	No
Dorst Creek	6,700	204	0	Yes
Lodgepole	6,700	204	0	Yes
Potwisha	2,100	40	0	Yes
South Fork	3,600	10	0	No
INSIDE KINGS CANYON NATIONAL PARK				
Azalea	6,500	110	0	No
Crystal Springs	6,500	50	0	No
Moraine	4,600	120	0	No
Sentinel	4,600	82	0	No
Sheep Creek	4,600	111	0	No
Sunset	6,500	157	0	No
OUTSIDE THE PARKS				
Big Meadows	7,600	25	0	No
Horse Creek	300	80	0	Yes
Hume Lake	5,200	74	0	No
Landslide	5,800	9	0	No
Lemon Cove	500	55	40	Yes
Princess	5,900	90	0	Yes
Stony Creek	6,400	49	0	No
Tenmile	5,800	13	0	No

restaurant, visitor center, children's nature center, evening ranger programs, and gift shop. From Giant Forest Museum, drive 5 miles northeast on the Generals Highway.

Dorst Creek Campground ★★, located 14 miles northwest of Giant Forest via the Generals Highway, is a high-elevation campground that offers easy access to Muir Grove and some pleasant backcountry trails. It has flush toilets and evening ranger programs. Group campsites are also available here by reservation.

In the Foothills area, the small **Potwisha Campground ★★** has well-spaced sites tucked beneath oak trees along the Marble Fork of the Kaweah River. The campground has flush

TOILETS	DRINKING WATER	SHOWERS	FIRE PITS/ GRILLS	LAUNDRY	RESERVATIONS POSSIBLE	FEES	OPEN
Yes	Yes	No	Yes	No	No	$12	Late May–Oct
Yes	Yes	No	Yes	No	No	$18	Apr–early Sept
Yes	Yes	No	Yes	No	No	$12	Late May–Oct
Yes	Yes	No	Yes	No	Yes	$20	Late June–mid-Sept
Yes	Yes	Yes	Yes	Yes	Yes	$18–$20	All year
Yes	Yes	No	Yes	No	No	$18	All year
Yes	No	No	Yes	No	No	$12	All year
Yes	Yes	Yes	Yes	No	No	$10–$18	All year
Yes	Yes	Yes	Yes	No	No	$18	May–Sept
Yes	Yes	Yes	Yes	Yes	No	$18	May–Oct
Yes	Yes	Yes	Yes	Yes	No	$18	Late Apr–Oct
Yes	Yes	Yes	Yes	Yes	No	$18	May–mid-Nov
Yes	Yes	Yes	Yes	Yes	No	$18	May–Sept
Yes	No	No	Yes	No	No	Free	Mid-May–Oct
Yes	Yes	Yes	Yes	No	Yes	$20	All year
Yes	Yes	No	Yes	No	Yes	$20	May–Oct
Yes	No	No	Yes	No	No	$16	May–Oct
Yes	Yes	Yes	Yes	Yes	Yes	$25–$40	All year
Yes	Yes	No	Yes	No	Yes	$18	Late May–Oct
Yes	Yes	Yes	Yes	No	Yes	$20	Late May–Oct
Yes	Yes	No	Yes	No	No	$16	Late May–Oct

toilets. Note that it does get hot in summer here. From the Ash Mountain Entrance, drive 3 miles northeast on the Generals Highway to the campground entrance.

The **Buckeye Flat Campground ★★**, which is open to tents only, is also set among oaks along the Middle Fork of the Kaweah River, and although it also gets hot in summer, it is among our favorites due to its scenic beauty. It has flush toilets. From the Ash Mountain Entrance, drive about 6 miles northeast on the Generals Highway to the Hanging Rock Picnic Area. From here, follow signs to the campground, which is several miles down a narrow, winding road.

South Fork Campground ★ is the smallest and most remote campground in the park, located just inside Sequoia's southwestern boundary. It is set along the South Fork of the Kaweah River and has vault toilets only. From the town of Three Rivers, go east on South Fork Road 23 miles to the campground. The campground is free during the winter season.

The two campgrounds in the Mineral King area are open to tents only—no RVs or trailers. **Atwell Mill Campground ★** is a small but pretty campground near the East Fork of the Kaweah River, at Atwell Creek. It has pit toilets. From Three Rivers, take Mineral King Road east for 20 miles to the campground. **Cold Springs Campground ★**, which also has vault toilets, is a beautiful place to stay—it's just not very accessible. Once you get here, however, you'll be rewarded with beautiful scenery. It's also a good starting point for many backcountry hikes, as it's near the Mineral King Visitor Center. From Three Rivers, take Mineral King Road east for 25 miles to the campground.

In Kings Canyon National Park

Some of the campgrounds in Kings Canyon are first come, first served only. Check www.nps.gov/seki/planyourvisit for reservations info on the others. All have flush toilets. Additional information can be obtained by calling the general Sequoia & Kings Canyon information line at ☏ **559/565-3341.**

In the Grant Grove area, there are three attractive campgrounds near the big trees: **Azalea ★**, **Crystal Springs ★**, and **Sunset ★**. All have a nice woodsy feel, are close to park facilities, and offer evening ranger programs. To get to them from the Big Stump Entrance, take CA 180 east about 1¾ miles.

Several pleasant campgrounds lie in the Cedar Grove Village area, all accessible from CA 180, and all close to the facilities in Cedar Grove Village. **Sentinel ★**, the first to open for the season, tends to fill up quickly. **Moraine ★** is the farthest from the crowds. **Sheep Creek ★**, located along picturesque Sheep Creek, is generally open from late spring to early fall. **Canyon View Campground ★** is for groups only.

Outside the Parks

The U.S. Forest Service operates campgrounds in **Giant Sequoia National Monument,** a 327,769-acre section of Sequoia National Forest, which was given national monument status by President Bill Clinton in April 2000. These sites provide a delightful forest camping experience and are usually less crowded than the national park campgrounds. There is also primitive camping available—no fee, no facilities.

In the Hume Lake area, all forest service campgrounds have pit toilets except the beautiful **Hume Lake Campground ★★**, which is set on the banks of the lake and has flush toilets. It's about 3 miles south of CA 180 via Hume Lake Road. The largest campground in this area is **Princess Campground ★★**, located along CA 180. Two smaller options, both beyond Hume Lake via Ten Mile Road, are **Landslide Campground ★** and **Tenmile Campground ★**.

In the Stony Creek/Big Meadows area, you'll find vault toilets at all U.S. Forest Service campgrounds except **Stony Creek Campground ★★**, located off Generals Highway in Stony Creek Village, which has flush toilets. Among the larger choices in this area is **Big Meadows Campground ★**, which is set along Big Meadows Creek. Nearby trails lead to the Jennie Lakes Wilderness. From Grant Grove Village, drive 7 miles southeast on the Generals Highway; then turn east on Big Meadows Road and drive 5 miles to the campground.

There are also several smaller, primitive campgrounds here; you can get information about the forest service campgrounds by contacting Giant Sequoia National Monument, Sequoia National Forest, Hume Lake Ranger District (② **559/338-2251**). You can make reservations at Hume Lake, Princess, or Stony Creek during the summer by calling ② **877/444-6777** or visiting www.recreation.gov.

Another great place to camp is **Horse Creek Campground ★★**, operated by the U.S. Army Corps of Engineers. It's located along the south shore of Lake Kaweah, in Lake Kaweah Recreation Area, about 6 miles east of the community of Lemon Cove off CA 198. The lake, which is about 5 miles long and a half-mile wide, covers 1,900 acres when full and is popular with boaters, who take to the water in kayaks, canoes, personal watercraft, fishing boats, and larger patio boats. There are several boat ramps, and boat rentals are available at the **Kaweah Marina** (www.kaweahmarina.com; ② **559/597-2526**); call for current rates and availability. This is also a popular fishing lake, where you're apt to catch largemouth bass, crappie, bluegill, catfish, and rainbow trout. The number of campsites varies with the water level, with the

---

Camping in Style

The luxury **Sequoia High Sierra Camp** ★★★ (www.sequoia highsierracamp.com; ☎ **866/654-2877**) in Giant Sequoia National Monument looks to one-up its Yosemite counterparts in terms of upscale "roughing it." For $250 per person, you get 330-square-foot bungalows with plush furnishings and three "California-cuisine-style" meals a day. Guests can choose to drive to a trail head and hike 1 mile or take an 11-mile trail to get there. For about $360 for one or two people (meals included; $75 extra for a third person), a less tony, but still quite civilized option is the **Bearpaw High Sierra Camp** ★★ (www.visit sequoia.com; ☎ **866/807-3598**), an 11-mile hike from Crescent Meadow in Sequoia National Park proper. Bearpaw is open June through September; Sequoia stays open into October.

---

fewest usually available in spring, when the lake is at its highest. Many sites are underwater here until mid-July. Some are shady sites and some open, and most have good views across the lake. Flush toilets are available. For information, contact the U.S. Army Corps of Engineers, Lake Kaweah Recreation Area (☎ **559/597-2301**). Campsite reservations are available by calling ☎ **877/444-6777** or visiting www.recreation.gov.

Those seeking a full-service commercial campground with RV hookups and all the usual amenities should head to **Lemon Cove/Sequoia Campground,** on the west side of Lemon Cove at 32075 Sierra Dr. (www.lemoncovesequoia camp.com; ☎ **559/370-4152**). This attractive and convenient campground, located in the foothills of the Sierra Nevada (22 miles east of U.S. 99), can handle both tents and large rigs with slide-outs. It offers cable TV hookups, propane sales, a convenience store, grassy and shaded sites, a recreation room, a playground and volleyball court, and an outdoor swimming pool.

WHERE TO EAT

Major improvements and additions to the restaurant scene in these parks in recent years mean that, yes, you can have a really good meal, or, if you prefer, find a quick and tasty lunch at a reasonable price. In addition, there are several good possibilities in the communities outside the parks, as well as within the Giant Sequoia National Monument.

Inside the Parks
MODERATE

Grant Grove Restaurant ★★ AMERICAN This attractively redesigned 8,000-square-foot restaurant now accommodates about 225 diners inside and outside; it formerly only held 74. The dining room is the primary option for a sit-down meal in the parks and is set in a busy area of Kings Canyon. Breakfast and lunch are typical American fare, with omelets, pancakes, French toast, etc. Lunch features sandwiches, burgers, and salads and dinner entrees include steaks, pastas, chicken, and trout dishes.

Grant Grove Village, Kings Canyon National Park. www.visitsequoia. com. ☏ **559/335-5500.** Breakfast and lunch $6.50–$14; lunch and dinner main courses $11–$30. Daily 7–10am, 11:30–9pm.

Peaks Restaurant ★ AMERICAN A wood-beamed ceiling, huge stone fireplace, and large windows offering wonderful views of the surrounding forest make this upscale lodge-style restaurant at Wuksachi Lodge a delightful spot for a refined and relaxing meal. Standard American breakfast buffets are the morning fare with burgers, salads, and sandwiches offered for lunch. The dinner entrees include chicken breast, grilled pork chops, pan-seared trout, and New York strip steak in 8- and 12-ounce sizes. There's a nice mix of meat and potatoes, seafood, and vegetarian fare.

Wuksachi Lodge, Sequoia National Park. www.visitsequoia.com. ☏ **559/625-7700.** Reservations suggested for dinner. Breakfast and lunch $12–$20; dinner main courses $15–$35. Daily 7–10am, 11:30am–3pm, and 5–10pm.

INEXPENSIVE

Cedar Grove Snack Bar ★ AMERICAN The only dining option at Cedar Grove offers a simple but adequate menu at affordable prices, although those staying at the lodge here for several days will quickly tire of the limited choices. The cafe has pleasant outdoor balcony seating that overlooks the river.

Cedar Grove, Kings Canyon National Park. www.visitsequoia.com. ☏ **559/565-3096.** Breakfast $7–$11; lunch and dinner main courses $6–$10. Mid-June to mid-Aug daily 7–10am, 11:30am–2:30pm and 5–9pm mid-May to mid-Oct. Closed mid-Oct to mid-May.

Lodgepole Market ★ GRILL   The Lodgepole Market Center—the park's biggest general store—sells groceries, camping supplies, snacks, and hot drinks. It also now contains Lodgepole Café, which serves a variety of grilled items for breakfast, lunch, and dinner. Pre-packaged grab-and-go items are also available, making it an easy stop for hikers and campers. Breakfast burritos and oatmeal are among the morning menu items. A variety of burgers, including a vegan option, as well as a grilled chicken sandwich, wild Alaskan cod sandwich, and beef hot dogs are on the menu.

Lodgepole, Sequoia National Park. www.visitsequoia.com/shop/lodgepole-market ✆ **559/565-3301.** Most items $4–$14. Daily 8am–8pm. Open year-round, with shorter hours fall–spring.

Silver City Mountain Resort ★ AMERICAN   This is your only option for a sit-down meal in Sequoia's remote Mineral King area, and it's a pretty good one, in spite of the lack of competition. The menu is basic, covering sandwiches and burgers, as well as dinner specials on weekend nights, but the homemade pie is the standout; try a slice of the Fruit of the Forest, with rhubarb, strawberries, apples, and blackberries.

Lodgepole, Sequoia National Park. www.silvercityresort.com. ✆ **559/561-3223.** Menu items $10–$18. Thurs–Mon 8am–8pm; Tues–Wed 8am–6pm. Closed Oct to Memorial Day.

Outside the Parks
EXPENSIVE
Vintage Press ★★ AMERICAN/CONTINENTAL   A good pick for a romantic dinner—or other special occasion—this stalwart's three dining rooms are elegant in the spirit of an upscale gin mill in Gold Rush–era San Francisco, featuring a handsome old bar imported from the city by the bay, plus many antiques and leaded mirrors. There's seasonal patio dining, too. The menu features several steaks alongside such dishes as Australian lobster tail and crispy veal sweetbreads with a port, jalapeño, and blue-cheese sauce. There are also exotic appetizers like escargot, goat-cheese *rellenos,* and sashimi. Lunch brings smaller steaks, sandwiches, and salads. The restaurant's wine cellar offers more than 1,000 selections.

216 N. Willis St., Visalia. www.thevintagepress.com. ✆ **559/733-3033.** Reservations recommended for dinner. Main courses $25–$55 lunch, $20–$40. Mon–Sat 11:30am–2pm and 5:30–10pm; Sun 10am–2pm and 5–9pm.

MODERATE

Gateway Restaurant and Lodge ★★★ AMERICAN
This old-school restaurant serves up great river views with its steaks and seafood. Located at the entrance to Sequoia National Park, the Gateway offers breakfast, lunch, and dinner daily. Choose from egg dishes, pancakes, and French toast for breakfast, or more elaborate fare during Sunday's champagne brunch. At lunch, the extensive menu includes more than 30 items, including sandwiches, burgers, and salads. For dinner, the menu is even longer, with pastas, meat, and seafood dishes, including chicken Marsala, scampi, New York pepper steak, rack of lamb, and trout.

45978 Sierra Dr., Three Rivers. www.gateway-sequoia.com. 🕐 **559/ 561-4133.** Breakfast $7–$23; brunch $26, lunch $8–$37; dinner $13–$85. Daily 8am–10pm. Bar open later.

Tommy's ★★ NEW AMERICAN   With a contemporary design and a menu to match, Tommy's is one of the most creative restaurants in Visalia. New owners have maintained most of the restaurant's traditions but have made some changes and added a Sunday brunch. The menu still reflects diverse influences from the South (in appetizers like fried sweet potatoes), the Far East (Kobe burgers), and Latin America (chili verde rib-eye). Most people enjoy the make-your-own s'mores for dessert, or try the award-winning bread pudding. The restaurant prides itself on its hand-cut Angus beef steaks, aged for at least 30 days, grilled, and finished with steak butter. There is a full bar and a California-centric wine list.

130 N. Encina St., Visalia. www.tommysdowntown.com. 🕐 **559/627-6077.** Lunch main courses $11–$15; dinner $18–$55, brunch $11–$14. Mon–Sat 11am–2pm, Sun 10am–2pm and 5–9pm. Bar open later.

INEXPENSIVE

Brewbaker's Restaurant & Brewery ★ BREWPUB
A noisy and fun microbrewery in downtown Visalia, Brewbaker's has a brass bar that's literally within arm's reach of the huge fermentation vats. Brick walls, stained glass, and a social vibe round out the atmosphere. The beers are well-made and delicious, while the food—including burgers, chili, fish and chips, and personal pizzas—is one of the best deals in town. Not only does this place brew beer, but it also makes its sodas in-house, in such flavors as orange and bubble gum.

There are seating areas upstairs and down, as well as on the second-story deck with a view out back.

219 E. Main St., Visalia. www.brewbakersbrewingco.com. ☎ **559/627-2739.** Main courses $11–$25. Daily 11:30am–10pm. Bar open later.

Ol' Buckaroo ★ AMERICAN   It all started with a food truck for T. R. Bousek and Nicky French, who set up shop originally on the Kaweah River in their Ol' Buckaroo food truck. Three years later they were ready for a brick-and-mortar restaurant and Buckaroo Diner was born in the original town saloon, rehabbed for 21st-century buckaroos. The fun-and-casual eatery pays tribute to Three Rivers' storied past while serving up small plates and healthy farm-to-table cuisine. Dine inside, in a sunroom overlooking the river or outside at picnic tables. Try the specialty, sweet tea–brined chicken, or Brandt Farm skirt steak or a fried chicken sandwich.

41695 Sierra Dr., Three Rivers. www.theolbuckaroo.com. ☎ **559/465-5088.** $11–$25. Sat–Mon 9:30am–1:30pm, 5:30–9pm; Thurs 5:30–9pm. Closed Tues–Wed.

Sierra Subs and Salads ★★ AMERICAN   Visitors probably don't expect to find a prize-winning sandwich shop in the tiny town of Three Rivers. But Sierra Subs and Salads is famous. Yelp reviewers like it so well that it consistently places in the Top 100 Best Places to Eat in the U.S. That's impressive, considering there are more than 616,000 restaurants nationwide. Yelp, which has been compiling the list of the 100 Best Places annually for several years, says a restaurant (or food truck) needs to have almost perfect 5-star ratings to make the list. Although locals say Sierra Subs is fine dining in a sandwich, the menu offers a lot more than subs. Diners find seven pizzas, seven quesadillas, 10 salads, and several other options such as grilled sandwiches, burgers and dogs, plus 15 vegetarian menu items. The restaurant makes its own sauces, salsas, soups, side salads, and vinaigrettes. Dine inside or at picnic tables by the river.

41717 Sierra Dr., Three Rivers. www.sierrasubsandsalads.com. ☎ **559/561-4810.** Sandwiches, salads, and subs $4–$9, pizzas $12–$18. Tues–Sat 10:30am–6pm, Sun 10:30am–3pm, closed Mon.

Picnic & Camping Supplies

Stores throughout the parks stock some basic camping supplies, such as flashlights, canteens, and tarps, plus enough food that you won't starve, but you'll find better selections in the nearby towns.

Within the parks, most of the stores are open daily from 7am until 10pm. The **Cedar Grove Market** is open May through October only, as is the **Lodgepole Market,** which has the widest selection available, including a good deli for takeout sandwiches (p. 140). The **Grant Grove Market** is open from 7am to 9pm May through October and from 9am to 6pm October through April. During the winter, a small selection of goods is available at **Wuksachi Lodge,** in Sequoia.

For the best selection and prices on foodstuffs outside the parks, stop in Visalia at **Save Mart,** 1591 E. Noble St., at CA 198 and Ben Maddox Way (② **559/622-0846**), on your way to the parks. This is an excellent supermarket with a good bakery and a deli that serves made-to-order sandwiches. Just east of it is a **Wal-Mart,** at 1819 E. Noble Ave. (② **559/636-2302**).

Camping supplies also can be purchased in Visalia at three large sporting goods stores: Big 5 Sporting Goods, 3637 S. Mooney Blvd. (www.big5sportinggoods.com; ② **559/308-7100**); Dick's Sporting Goods, 3637 S Mooney Blvd. (www.dickssportinggoods.com; ② **559/636-0633**); Sportsman's Warehouse, 1650 W. Visalia Pkwy (www.sportsmans.com; ② **559/308-7100**).

8

WHERE TO STAY & EAT IN SEQUOIA & KINGS CANYON | Where to Eat

A NATURE GUIDE TO YOSEMITE AND SEQUOIA & KINGS CANYON NATIONAL PARKS

9

Yosemite, Sequoia & Kings Canyon provide an astonishing variety of everything you hope to find in national parks: vistas and close-ups; isolation and community; wonderment and familiarity. John Muir's foresight in calling for the preservation of America's natural treasures has morphed into the stewardship of the women and men who today fight to protect and improve this legacy.

THE LANDSCAPE

Towering sheets of granite. Lush forests that give way to emerald meadows blanketed in wildflowers. Views that stretch farther than some countries and make visitors feel like they are standing on the edge of the world. Yosemite has an almost bizarre conglomeration of sheer granite monoliths and wide-open spaces. Sequoia & Kings Canyon have trees that are as wide at the base as some homes, along with wildflowers in almost every patch of sun. All these wonders occur because of the area's astounding geological nature.

About 300 million years ago, layers of sediment that had been building up on the ocean floor were forced under the emerging North American continent. The process created such intense heat that the sediment became molten magma, some of which erupted via volcanoes. Where it chilled and hardened before reaching the surface, the magma created huge slabs of granite.

This process continued intermittently for about 150 million years, forming a large mountain range roughly parallel to the West Coast—the Sierra Nevada. For the next 55 million years, wind and water ate away at the volcanoes and sedimentary rock, sweeping it into California's Central Valley and leaving mountains of exposed granite.

Scientists theorize earthquakes along the present-day San Andreas Fault began forcing the eastern edge of a landmass beneath the Sierra about 25 million years ago, eventually tipping west, raising tall mountain peaks. In Yosemite, the upheaval raised the park's eastern range to 11,000 feet. In Sequoia & Kings Canyon, it created the ominously barren and beautiful Kaweah Ridge, also known as the Great Western Divide, which ranges from about 11,000 to 14,000 feet in elevation.

As rivers raged through the valleys, they carved deeper and deeper into the earth, eroding the bedrock. Great canyons were formed, and when the earth's temperature cooled about 3 million years ago, glaciers covered the Sierra Nevada. These fields of ice tore at the granite, expanding and contracting with such force that they carved deep valleys, slicing granite walls vertically into the steep U-shapes of Yosemite Valley and Kings Canyon.

Rock Formations

When the glaciers melted, they left behind steep mountains smoothed by ice, along with piles of debris that dammed the flow of rivers, creating lakes in the valleys. The rest of the landscaping took place in an evolutionary blink of an eye. Over the course of 10,000 years, sediment, swept down from above, filled these lakes. Meadows were formed, and then came wildflowers, followed by trees, and eventually people.

You can still see **glaciers** in Yosemite, near Tuolumne Meadows. Also check out the glaciers on Yosemite's Mount Lyell, Mount Dana, and Mount Maclure. The glaciers here were probably formed about 2,500 years ago but are quickly receding today.

Glaciers are responsible for the variety of **rock formations** in the parks. There are spires, domes, sheets, and arches. Yosemite has cornered the market for number and diversity, offering one or more of each within the span of an easy 3-mile walk. Most of the unusual rock landmarks here were created by fractures within the rock. These fractures occur vertically, horizontally, and at an incline. Called **joints,** they represent the weakest point of a rock and a point that has already been broken. The type of joint most common in Yosemite, and evident in Sequoia & Kings Canyon, is *sheeting.* Concentric joints—fractures that seem to occur along curved lines—form after years of increasing and decreasing pressure from overlaying rock. When pressure decreases, the granite expands upward and breaks or fractures off in sheets, like peeling an onion very slowly.

Erratic boulders are another common sight. These large rocks were originally located elsewhere but were transported and plopped down haphazardly—again, probably by glaciers.

Ridges of rocky deposits are called **moraines,** left behind as glaciers recede. The best place to see moraines is in Yosemite, en route from Tuolumne Meadows to Tioga Pass.

The most famous rocks in Yosemite are Half Dome and El Capitan. Although **Half Dome** was probably never a full dome like North Dome, which it faces, geologists believe that about 20% of the original rock was sheared off by glaciers. The face looks smooth and slippery but is filled with ledges and ridges, making it a rock climber's paradise. Similar ridges exist on the dome side, enabling hikers to climb to the top (see p. 43). Although it looks small, the top measures 13 acres. Half Dome is 8,842 feet above sea level and towers roughly 4,800 feet above the valley floor, the highest point in Yosemite Valley.

El Capitan is on the left, or north, side of the valley as you enter. It rises 3,593 feet above the valley floor and 7,569 feet above sea level. Toward the top of El Cap, the slope of the rock increases and hangs over the valley floor. Called the nose, it's a challenge for rock climbers. Look for climbers on the face, as well as off to the sides of El Cap; it's where many experts ascend, and beginners learn the ropes. It takes around 4 to 7 days to climb El Capitan. The first climber reached the summit in 1958, after 47 days. And on June 3, 2017, 31-year-old Alex Honnold accomplished the unthinkable: He completed the first free solo climb of El Cap, reaching the summit in 3 hours and 56 minutes without any safety equipment.

To the east of El Cap are the **Three Brothers**—three outcroppings of rock called Lower Brother, Middle Brother, and Eagle Peak. The rocks appear to be riding piggyback and were formed by parallel fractures on an incline.

The **Cathedral Spires** are directly opposite El Cap, on the other side of the valley. They will appear before you if you turn your back to El Cap and look carefully—the rock is almost camouflaged by the valley wall beyond. Somehow these, and other spires in the park, have withstood nature's evolutionary barrage.

Another spire, this one known as **Lost Arrow,** is east of Yosemite Falls, below Yosemite Point. Look for the waterfalls to the north of Yosemite Lodge. The outcropping of rock to the east is **Yosemite Point.** Lost Arrow is an independent spire in the same area.

Continue moving east to see the **Royal Arches,** a series of 1,500-foot half-circles carved out of the rock, to the north of the Ahwahnee Hotel. Here, the material that was once above the arches eroded away, taking pressure off the rock below, which expanded and cracked parallel to the surface. During particularly wet springs, water cascades over the arches in great sheets.

Above the arches is **North Dome,** the smooth, slightly lopsided dome mentioned earlier. It rises 3,562 feet above the valley floor. Nearby is **Washington Column,** a spire with a tip 1,920 feet above the valley floor. Ahwahnee Indian legend has it that a man and woman who lived in the valley long ago fought so often that it upset the spirits. The unhappy couple was turned to stone and separated by Tenaya Creek. He is North Dome, with Washington Column as his walking stick. She is Half Dome, and if you look at it closely, a woman's profile faces northeast. Legend also has it that the streak of lighter rock between her cheek and nose was caused by a stream of tears.

Domes and impressive geologic formations appear outside the valley as well. Most are in Yosemite's high country, en route to Tuolumne Meadows, and foremost is **Olmsted Point,** an overlook that gives visitors a chance to see the granite Tenaya Canyon. Cloud's Rest and the rear of Half

Dome are two distinct shapes easily recognizable from Olmsted Point, which is 9 miles west of Tuolumne Meadows.

Tuolumne Meadows itself is ringed with domes and peaks, many of which are an easier climb than the ones rising above the valley.

In Sequoia National Park, **Moro Rock** is a dome towering 6,725 feet above sea level. Moro Rock's summit offers breathtaking views of the Kaweah Ridge, with some peaks rising to 14,000 feet.

Kings Canyon National Park boasts **North Dome,** above Cedar Grove. Some people with a vivid imagination say it resembles Half Dome. North Dome is not accessible by car or on foot.

Waterfalls

Waterfalls hang over the Yosemite Valley like a sparkling diamond necklace. The valley boasts three of the world's tallest waterfalls. Upon entering the valley, you'll spot the 620-foot **Bridalveil Fall** first. It looks large, but that's because you haven't seen the rest of the cast.

The real biggie is **Yosemite Falls,** close to Yosemite Lodge. The fall appears to be one drop but is, in fact, a set of waterfalls that measures a combined 2,425 feet. Lower Yosemite Fall drops 320 feet, Upper Yosemite Fall descends 1,430 feet, and a cascade in the middle makes up the difference.

To the west of El Capitan you'll find **Ribbon Fall,** which drops an uninterrupted 1,612 feet to the valley floor but is often dry in summer.

The longest single fall in Yosemite is **Sentinel Fall.** It drops 2,000 feet from the west side of Sentinel Rock, directly across the valley floor from Yosemite Falls. To view this waterfall, walk back toward El Cap and make an about-face—it's one of the geology-obscured views in the park.

Up the valley are a series of dramatic staircase falls accessible only on foot. **Vernal Fall** and **Nevada Fall** occur just a half-mile apart along the same river.

Waterfalls in Sequoia & Kings Canyon are less numerous but still impressive. **Mist Falls,** in Kings Canyon, is beautiful but requires a 4-mile hike (p. 117). This wide waterfall near Cedar Grove is up a rushing creek, which includes several large cascades.

THE LIFE & TIMES OF john muir

Over the course of his illustrious 75 years, John Muir earned a nickname: "Father of Our National Parks." In the late 19th century, he pushed for conservation of the pristine wilderness and helped establish Yosemite and Sequoia & Kings Canyon as national parks.

Born in Scotland in 1838, Muir emigrated with his family to Wisconsin at the age of 11. After an accident nearly blinded him about a decade later, he dropped everything to pursue his fascination with the natural world and decided to go to the Amazon—on foot. He didn't make it, but traveling became a way of life for Muir, and his journeys eventually took him west. He discovered the Sierra Nevada area in 1868 and worked as a shepherd in the Yosemite area. He later ran a sawmill nearby.

Muir began writing about the Sierra Nevada the moment he arrived, and his passionate words started finding an audience in the late 1800s. He wrote books, contributed to numerous periodicals, and became a leading voice in the budding environmentalist movement. In 1892, Muir helped found the Sierra Club. In 1903, he took Teddy Roosevelt camping in the Yosemite backcountry and catalyzed Roosevelt's vision of an entire system of national parks.

Muir is a legend not only for his words and his deeds, but also because he was something of an eccentric. He never shaved, making way for an impressive beard. He experienced nature to its fullest—he climbed a tree during an incredible storm, sledded down Yosemite Valley's steep walls on his rump to avoid an avalanche, and chased a bear so he could study the animal's stride. (Not surprisingly, these actions have since been banned by the National Park Service.)

From the first moment a politician pondered Hetch Hetchy Reservoir, Muir fought it. Damming and drowning a place of such beauty—it was said to rival that of Yosemite Valley—was sacrilege to him. But San Francisco needed water to drink, and Congress passed legislation approving Hetch Hetchy Reservoir in 1913. John Muir died the very next year—some say of a broken heart.

Below is **Roaring River Fall,** a length of waterfall also accessible only on foot; it flows from Cloud and Deadman canyons. **Garlic Fall,** in the Monarch Wilderness area just outside Kings Canyon, can be viewed from the Yucca Point overlook on CA 180.

Note: Most waterfalls are fed by snowmelt and rely on winter runoff to survive. In late summer, many of them (including Yosemite Falls) dry up.

THE FLORA

There are more than 1,500 types of plants in Yosemite, Sequoia & Kings Canyon, and describing them all would fill this book. With species ranging from tiny lichen to giant sequoias, the flora in the parks is similar, varying primarily by elevation.

Trees

The trees native to the region consist mostly of conifers and broadleaf trees. Conifers have needles and cones, do not shed during cooler months, and maintain their green year-round, earning the name *evergreen.* Broadleaf trees drop their leaves in fall and bloom anew in spring.

Ponderosa Pine

At lower elevations, the two most common pines you'll find are the ponderosa pine and Jeffrey pine (both also known as "yellow pines"). The **ponderosa pine** has yellow-orange bark, needles grouped in threes, and bark scales that fit together like a jigsaw puzzle. The trunk of a ponderosa pine can grow up to 6 feet in diameter. The **Jeffrey pine** is like the ponderosa but tends to live at higher elevations.

Jeffrey Pine

The **sugar pine** grows at slightly higher elevations and can be seen along many hikes. These pines produce large pinecones, have short needles grouped in fives, and have a reddish-brown bark. Trunks can grow to almost 7 feet in diameter, and mature trees sport very crooked branches.

Sugar Pine

Pines found at higher elevations include the lodgepole and whitebark.

The **lodgepole pine,** the most widely distributed pine in North America, groups its needles in twos; it has yellow-orange bark and small cones.

Lodgepole Pine

Firs are another species of conifer found in the parks. **Red firs,** with short needles that curl up and cones ranging from 5 to 8 inches, are found at elevations of 6,000 to 9,000 feet, while **white firs** are found at lower elevations. Wildlife often take refuge in the large cavities near the base of old trunks. Both firs grow in forests near Yosemite's Glacier Point and in the high country along Tioga Road.

Red Fir

At the highest elevations (9,000–14,000 ft.), look for **foxtail pines,** gnarled trees that have adapted to the harsh rocky life of living at the top. This pine, like the whitebark pine, looks stunted and warped, often with a twisted trunk and spiky, dead-looking top. The roots grow over granite and require only a short growing season, allowing the tree to cling to a frigid existence.

Foxtail Pine

Incense cedar is often confused with the giant sequoias, as both have reddish shaggy bark that almost crumbles to the touch. But an incense cedar has flat sprays of foliage that emit a fragrant smell in warm weather and small reddish-brown cones resembling a duck's bill when opened.

Incense Cedar

The undisputed heavyweight of the national parks' flora is the **giant sequoia.** Smaller ones can be hard to identify, but there is no mistaking a mature 250-foot tree dating back 2,000 to 3,000 years. These trees grow to a

Giant Sequoia

height of 311 feet, weigh 2.7 million pounds, and can have a base 40 feet in diameter. Tree limbs can reach 8 feet in diameter. The trees are bare until about 100 to 150 feet up and then sprout branches. The bark, naturally fire resistant, ranges from 4 to 24 inches thick. These trees resist decay and produce abundant small cones with hundreds of seeds the size of oatmeal flakes. Interestingly, it takes a fire to dry the cones out enough to release the seeds.

Giant sequoias can be found at elevations ranging from 5,000 to 7,500 feet, and occasionally as low as 3,500 feet. Obviously, the best place to see these trees is throughout Sequoia & Kings Canyon National Parks. The large stands of Giant Forest and Grant Grove offer fantastic, easily accessible examples of giant sequoias, and there are other groves, accessible by foot, scattered throughout the park. Yosemite has three stands of giant sequoias—the Mariposa Grove near Wawona, and the smaller Tuolumne and Merced groves near the Big Oak Flat Entrance.

Flowering Plants

Wildflowers produce an array of colors during spring and summer, as they peek from cracks and crevices or carpet fields and meadows. The blooming season begins in February in the lowlands, lasting into early fall in the high country. The list of wildflowers found in these parks is intimidating and includes more than 50 species, some of which are described below.

Lupine

Splashed on meadows and along hillsides is a lavender flower, **lupine.** It's easily recognized by its palmate leaves—leaves that originate from a central point like fingers from a hand. Look for the bloom along valley floors and in the Wawona region of Yosemite. You will also see **cow parsnip** here, bluish-tinged flowers set on spindly stems, with almost fernlike leaves. The cow parsnip's dartlike flowers resemble violets at a distance, but closer inspection reveals an umbrella-shaped top and leafless stalk.

Cow Parsnip

You may also see monkey flower and yarrow at these elevations. The **monkey flower** is one of nature's brightest flowers, ranging from blue to purple, pink, and orange, and seen along streams and at high altitudes in gravelly soil. Petals consist of two-lipped blossoms that more imaginative folk say resemble the smiling face of a monkey. Growing up to 3 feet tall, **yarrow** blooms as a flat, wide cluster of white (occasionally pink) flowers with a pungent aroma. It was used by Native Americans as a healing herb, a drink to cure indigestion and to reduce fever. Today the dried flower is commonly seen in potpourri.

Monkey Flower

Yarrow

At night, look for **evening primrose**—its four-petal flowers open at sunset and wilt in the morning, and are pollinated by moths. Blossoms range from white to yellow and pink and have a sweet lemon smell; stems can reach 6 feet.

Evening Primrose

One of the last flowers of the season is **meadow goldenrod,** which appears in late summer and fall. The plant grows in long stalks, with narrow leaves protruding all along it, and may be topped by a shock of yellow that resembles a feather. Goldenrod was used by American Indians to cure all sorts of ailments.

Meadow Goldenrod

In forests, you'll find pussy paws and snow plant in the shade, and lupine, mariposa lily, and mountain violet in the sun. The **mariposa lily,** which blooms beneath pines in Yosemite, is named for the Spanish

Mariposa Lily

word for butterfly, which it is said to resemble. Blooms consist of three snow-white petals with dark spots at their base; the long stems give the flowers a floating appearance. American Indians roasted the bulbs of these blooms to eat.

At higher and cooler elevations, the **meadow penstemon** produces a group of bright pink flowers atop a single, slender stalk. The blooms are arranged like trumpets, pointing in every direction.

Meadow Penstemon

A favorite flower of humming-birds, **columbine** grows in meadows and springs from rocky crevices. It looks quite fragile, with bushy leaves clumped at the base of bare stalks that produce droopy blooms. The color can vary, but look for five petals that extend backward in a long, pointed tube.

Columbine

Shrubs & Plants

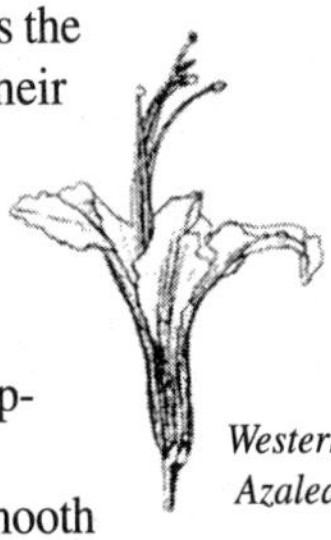

One of the many plants found in the parks is the wild azalea. These plants resemble their household cousins and are often the first to proclaim the arrival of spring, with an abundance of vibrant color. The Sierra sports just one variety: the **western azalea,** a low-lying shrub with smooth, deep-green leaves.

Western Azalea

The **mariposa manzanita,** with its smooth red-to-purple bark and oval, coin-size leaves, blooms year-round and is but one type of manzanita common in this region. The mariposa manzanita produces small white and pink clusters of flowers that eventually turn into berries that look like little apples, which is what *manzanita* means in Spanish. This shrub is plentiful in the foothills of Sequoia National Park.

Mariposa Manzanita

A common pest is **poison oak,** prevalent below 5,000 feet. Watch for a shrub with shiny three-leaf clusters and white berries. In winter, poison-oak stems are bare and very difficult to recognize, so steer clear of any thickets that resemble sticks stuck in the ground.

Poison Oak

THE FAUNA

Think of the parks as nature's zoo. There are no cages, no man-made habitats—just wide-open spaces with enough room for more than 200 species of mammals and birds, some of which are described below.

Birds

The Sierra Nevada is a bird-watcher's paradise. Each year, 135 species visit Yosemite Valley alone. The most treasured of the area's feathered friends include the great horned owl, the peregrine falcon, and the California condor, all of which send birdwatchers into ornithological ecstasy.

You're more likely to hear the **great horned owl** than see one. Its hoots sound like sonar, but since it is nocturnal, it's difficult to spot. If you happen to hear it, try to locate its branch first, and then the bird: It has large tufts of feathers near both ears. But don't get disheartened if you search in vain—these birds are great ventriloquists.

You'll have more luck observing a pair of

Great Horned Owl

nesting **peregrine falcons** on El Capitan or Glacier Point, although you'll need binoculars. For several years now, the birds have made this their own personal day-care center, hatching and raising their young on narrow ledges before beginning flight instruction. One of four falcon species in the park, the peregrine falcon is marked by a hood of dark feathers from head to back, contrasting against lighter

Peregrine Falcon

feathers underneath. This bird is a wizard in flight, reaching speeds of up to 200 mph mid-dive. It was removed from the endangered species list around the turn of the century.

Still endangered is the **California condor,** the largest land bird in North America, with a 9-foot wingspan. The birds can glide 10 miles at a time without flapping their wings. Keen eyesight allows them to spot a dead animal carcass from miles away. Their numbers dropped below 40 in 1975, due to pesticide use and the loss of habitat to construction projects. A pair of condors can raise only one young

California Condor

every 2 years. In the 1980s, the remaining birds were captured and placed in zoos, where the young were hand-reared. Then some of the adolescent birds were released into the wild and have been seen occasionally in Kings Canyon. Today about 275 California condors exist in the wild.

In both Yosemite and Sequoia & Kings Canyon, the birds you're most likely to see are the American robin, Steller's jay, acorn woodpecker, northern flicker, band-tailed pigeon, two varieties of blackbird, sparrow, swift, American dipper, belted kingfisher, duck, warbler, brown creeper, mountain chickadee, and red-breasted and white-breasted nuthatches.

Yosemite Valley is a great place to see many of these species because its environment includes streambeds, rivers, forest, and meadowlands, often within the space of a city block. A stroll anywhere along the Merced River should take you within visual distance of all these birds, whose habitats include the water, meadows, and adjacent forests.

A reddish-orange breast easily distinguishes the **American robin.** These are the same birds you can see back home throughout much of North America, in suburbs and backyards, building cup-shaped nests on windowsills or the ledges of buildings. Before the bird adapted to urban living, it preferred a woodland habitat. It has long been considered a harbinger of spring, but in reality some of these birds stay put year-round. The precocious **Steller's jay** is unfazed by humans, it is a bold beggar, landing on picnic tables and elsewhere near food,

American Robin

Steller's Jay

while letting loose a screech that could wake the dead. The Steller's jay is bright blue, with a dark head and prominent crest. This bird is also capable of a beautiful soft warble.

Like the Steller's jay, you're likely to hear the **woodpecker** before you see it—listen for its methodical rata-tat-tat. Woodpeckers can also emit a startling call that sounds like "wack-up." Woodpeckers are distinguished by black-and-white markings and a red crown, with an occasional bit of yellow. The **northern flicker** is also a woodpecker—look for a brown-feathered bird clinging to the side of a tree. Its wings have a reddish tinge and it sports a red mustache. This bird prefers to feed on the ground, where it searches for ants. **Band-tailed pigeons** are similar to their city-dwelling cousins but prefer tall forest trees to buildings.

Northern Flicker

Band-Tailed Pigeon

In meadowlands, you will likely see sparrows, the black-headed grosbeak, the uncommon western tanager—a bird with fluorescent feathers—and two varieties of blackbird. The **Brewer's blackbird** and the **red-winged blackbird** both make their home here. Brewer's blackbirds nest in trees, while their red-winged relatives prefer slightly marshy areas. The **black-headed grosbeak** has black, white, and orange markings, and a distinctive beak used for cracking seeds. Its soft, lyrical warble is music compared to those of other valley dwellers, and this bird is considered a sure sign of spring. The easy-to-spot **western tanager** is bright yellow with a reddish-orange head and is frequently observed in Yosemite Valley during spring and summer.

Black-Headed Grosbeak

Western Tanager

If you're near moving water, you might search for American dippers, belted kingfishers, ducks, and warblers. The **American dipper** is notable more for its flying acrobatics than for its

American Dipper

nondescript color. The bird flies headfirst into the river to walk upstream along the bottom, clinging to rocks in its search for food. The **belted kingfisher** is a highly visible blue bird that flies low over water in search of prey. You may see it perched

Belted Kingfisher

above the water, clinging to branches and underbrush, and keeping a watchful eye out for insects and fish. It has a reddish band on its chest and a noticeable crest up top. The call of the kingfisher is distinctive: loud, rattling, and clicking.

In the forests live brown creepers, mountain chickadees, and red- and white-breasted nuthatches. The **brown creeper** is difficult to spot because of the camouflage feathers that disguise it among tree trunks. Small, with a slender, curved beak, the creeper usually begins foraging for insects at the base of a tree and works its way up, clinging to the bark with razor-sharp claws. The **mountain chickadee** is another songbird with a delightful melody that sounds like "chickadee-dee-dee." These tiny, friendly, hyperactive birds have dark caps and bibs, a gray or brown back, and a distinctive white eyebrow. They nest in woodpecker holes or other small tree holes. **Nuthatches** are the birds you'll see walking headfirst down a tree trunk—no simple feat. Also called upside-down birds, the red-breasted and white-breasted versions are aptly described by their names. They are partial to abandoned woodpecker holes.

Brown Creeper

Mountain Chickadee

Nuthatch

And let's not forget the **swift,** almost always found in flight above Yosemite Valley. These birds spend more time air-bound than any other land bird. When they do stop, they cling to vertical surfaces because their tiny feet are unsuitable for perches. Look up to see swifts flying between Yosemite's great granite walls.

In the Wawona region south of Yosemite Valley, you'll find the bushtit and wrentit, scrub jay, California thrasher, yellow warbler, lesser goldfinch, barn swallow, and ash-throated and rare willow flycatchers. The **yellow warbler** is the more colorful version of the warbler described above. **Flycatchers** are better known for their insect-hunting abilities than for distinctive markings. The **willow flycatcher** is an endangered species and has gray, brown, and olive plumage. All flycatchers are very territorial. **Goldfinches,** sometimes referred to as wild canaries, are gregarious birds, with bright colors and cheerful songs.

Yellow Warbler

Willow Flycatcher

Bushtit

Wrentit

Bushtits spend most of the year in flocks of about 20, constantly twittering at each other with a soft, lisping call. These acrobatic fliers are small, grayish birds with tiny bills. **Wrentits** are secretive birds—hard to see but easy to hear. They seldom venture far from home and prefer to live in chaparral or scrub thickets. Once mated, they form devoted pairs, constantly pruning and preening each other. When seen close together, they resemble a single ball of gray fluff.

The high country of Yosemite and Sequoia & Kings Canyon attracts dozens more birds, drawn by altitude and mountain meadows, including the dark-eyed junco, kestrel, red-tailed hawk, killdeer, Williamson's sapsucker, Clark's nutcracker, and ptarmigan.

Juncos, often referred to as snowbirds, are common visitors to bird feeders. Small and friendly, these birds resemble the sparrow, which also frequents this region. But the dark-eyed junco has a pink bill, white-to-bluish underbelly, and dark feathers from the crown down its back, and can usually be seen hopping along the

Junco

ground in search of food. The *Killdeer*
killdeer—named for its shrill
call, is a performer, often feign-
ing a broken wing to ward intrud-
ers off when they venture too near its
nest. And no wonder—nests are little
more than a shallow depression in the
ground lined with pebbles. Adult killdeer have two black
bands across their throats, while chicks have one.

Killdeer

Sapsuckers are specialized woodpeckers
that extract the sap from trees with their
brush-tipped tongues after drilling holes
with their beaks. They also eat insects
attracted to the sap. The **Williamson's
sapsucker** strongly resembles the northern flicker described above, minus the
red mustache. **Nutcrackers** are bold
cousins of the crow family. **Clark's nutcrackers** specialize in prying seeds from
pine cones and make forests their stamp-
ing grounds. In late summer and fall, the
birds begin hoarding seeds for
winter, tucking them in a pouch
under their tongue during
transport to slopes, where
they poke holes in the
ground and bury their treasure. A single nutcracker
can hide 30,000 seeds. More
remarkable is the fact that
they remember where the
stock is buried by the position
of nearby landmarks, even when the ground is covered with
snow. Clark's nutcracker resembles a crow, with a gray head
and body and black wings tipped with white.

*Williamson's
Sapsucker*

*Clark's
Nutcracker*

Finally, the **ptarmigan** is a unique
bird, well adapted to changing seasons in cold climates. These small,
stocky grouse have mottled brown
feathers in summer to help camouflage them against the rocky moun-
taintops where they live, but the

Ptarmigan

feathers turn pure white in winter to match the snow. Like all grouse, ptarmigans have feathered legs, and in winter their feet are also covered with feathers. During the spring mating season, males sport a vibrant red comb and strut in short flights while cackling, all to attract a mate.

In addition to the above birds, Hammond's flycatcher, Cassin's finch, common flicker, pine sparrow, chipping sparrow, white-crowned sparrow, and violet-green swallow are all prevalent in the high country.

Mammals

Mammals in these parks are not seen as often as birds, and therefore, they're a lot more fun to spot. Most common are the mule deer, raccoon, squirrel, chipmunk, fox, coyote, and black bear. At higher elevations, you may also see Belding ground squirrels and Douglas's squirrels, yellow-bellied marmots, pikas, pine martens, badgers, mountain lions, bobcats, porcupines, long-tailed weasels, striped and spotted skunks, and northern water shrew.

Mule deer are most frequently seen grazing in meadows at dawn and dusk. Although they seem gentle enough, mule deer should be treated with the same reverence accorded any wild animal: Give them a wide berth and, of course, refrain from feeding them. Many injuries have been recorded against humans who attempt to get close or feed them. The mule deer is named for its large, mulelike ears, and adults can weigh up to 200 pounds, surviving on a mix of grasses, leaves, tender twigs, and herbs. Males grow antlers for use during the mating season. And no, it is not true that the age of a male deer can be gauged by counting the points on its antlers.

A variety of members of the squirrel family reside in this region, including chipmunks and marmots. The most common is the **California gray squirrel,** often seen in trees with its gray coat and bushy tail. **Douglas's squirrel,** common in Sequoia, is an olive-to-rust or gray color, with

Mule Deer

Douglas's Squirrel

a reddish underbelly. There are at least
five different varieties of **chipmunks**
in this region. Smaller than squirrels, they're quick and love to chat-
ter, especially when scolding those
who venture too near. Chipmunks

Chipmunk

range in color from reddish-brown to brownish-gray, and all
varieties have four stripes running the length of their backs.

At higher elevations, you'll
find the **yellow-bellied marmot.** Resembling woodchucks,
they regularly sunbathe and
can tease visitors into
believing they are tame.

*Yellow-Bellied
Marmot*

They're not. Adult marmots appear yel-
lowish-brown, weigh up to 5 pounds,
reach 15 to 18 inches in length, emit a
high-pitched shrill as a warning, and
live beneath rock piles or tree roots.

Porcupine

The **porcupine** is a unique rodent.
These short, stock-legged creatures
are covered from head to toe with
quills that detach at the touch, piercing whomever or whatever touches them. Each animal carries about 30,000 quills
that serve as a serious deterrent to all but the stupidest predators. Porcupines sleep during the day and forage at night,
curling into a ball when approached by a would-be predator.
In spring, females produce one offspring, which is born with
soft quills (thankfully) that harden within minutes.

Pikas look like a cross between a rodent and
a hare and are distant relatives of the rabbit
family. Pikas have oversize ears, although
they're proportionately much smaller
than those found on their cousins and
live in colonies above the tree line
throughout the West. They scamper
over rocks and emit a high-pitched
squeal whenever a predator is sighted.

Pika

Raccoons are considered pests in sub-
urbia, but in the wild they are shy
nocturnal animals, easily spotted by

Raccoon

their ringed tails and the appearance of a black mask across their eyes. Some are no bigger than a large house cat, but males can grow to be 3 feet in length and may weigh more than 40 pounds. These animals are adaptive, eating everything from fish and small rodents to fruit, nuts, and earthworms.

The parks contain a large number of weasel-family members, including badgers, martens, skunks, and what most people know as weasels. The badger and marten are distant cousins of the weasel. **Badgers** can reach up to 2 feet in length and weigh up to 25 pounds. This heavy, short-legged animal has black feet, black-and-white face markings, and coarse yellowish-gray fur.

Badger

If you're not familiar with skunks, consider yourself fortunate. Best known for the awful scent they release when scared or under attack, skunks are otherwise cute, fluffy animals with distinctive black-and-white markings. Most common is the **striped skunk,** its white-on-black stripe running from nose to tail tip. The **spotted skunk** is rarer but lives in Sequoia & Kings Canyon National Parks.

Striped Skunk

Foxes, coyotes, black bears, bobcats, and mountain lions also inhabit this region. Most avoid crowds and shun humans, but coyotes and black bears are frequently spotted in the middle of Yosemite Valley, where they rely on the misguided benevolence of humans who feed them. **Coyotes** resemble dogs, with long gray fur and bushy tails. They feed primarily on small rodents and the occasional fawn and grow to weigh between 25 and 30 pounds. One of the coyote's most distinctive traits is its howl, a long, haunting call that some consider frightening.

Coyote

The **black bear** is the largest mammal in these parks. It is often confused with the grizzly bear, which is much larger and much more fearsome. Incidents involving black bears usually occur due to improper food storage. *Never* feed bears, and by no

Black Bear

means should you walk toward them. Observe from a safe distance. Despite their names, black bears can also be brown, blond, and cinnamon colored. Adult black bears grow to 250 to 500 pounds, and larger ones have been recorded. They are omnivores, eating both meat and vegetation, and they've proved very adaptable to hot dogs, hamburgers, and cookies. Unfortunately, once they become dependent on human food, these bears can prove bold and determined to continue their new diet. At this point, they must be trapped and killed by park rangers. Therefore, you *must* follow food-storage regulations.

Foxes, bobcats, and mountain lions are less frequently spotted in the parks, especially the latter two. The most common fox is the **gray fox,** with its bushy tail, reddish-gray coat, and black paws. Members of the dog family, they look larger than they are—average weight is 10 pounds. Foxes are skillful hunters and eat rodents, berries, rabbits, and insects. **Bobcats** inhabit Sequoia & Kings Canyon National Parks. They are nocturnal and resemble a large cat, with a black-spotted tawny coat. The "bob" refers to their stub of a tail, a feature shared with their close relative, the

Gray Fox

Bobcat

lynx. Adults max out at
about 20 pounds, and
while much smaller
than the next predator
on our list, bobcats can
kill deer many
times their size.
They are masters
of the slow hunt—

Mountain Lion

methodical, solitary, and patient. **Mountain lions** shy away
from any human contact, so seeing one is extremely rare.
These large cats can reach 5 feet in length. Their fur ranges
from tawny to gray, their tails tipped with black. Solitary
predators that prefer elk and deer, they'll settle for a porcupine or skunk in lean times.

THE ECOSYSTEM

Quite often, the ravages of nature are the forces of change,
and such has been the case in these national parks. Recent
rockslides and floods have reestablished nature's supremacy,
and preservation efforts and long-term studies have been
underway for more than a decade.

In Yosemite, the return of the peregrine falcon was her-
alded as a milestone. When birdwatchers counted three nesting pairs and five offspring in 1996, the news traveled across
the nation.

Considerable attention is going toward restoring meadows,
limiting trails, and bringing back native plants pushed out by
the impact of humans. The valley has seen the reseeding of a
black-oak forest along the bikeway between Yosemite Village and Yosemite Falls, while controversy regarding its
future (as well as that of Hetch Hetchy) rages on.

Large boulders placed in the Merced River long ago by
settlers and early park managers changed the course of the
waterway and created unnatural swimming holes. These are
being removed, and the river is being allowed to pursue its
own direction. Volunteers are also working to repair damage
done by hikers who step off the trails.

In Sequoia & Kings Canyon, fire management has been a
major concern since the 1960s, when the park policies began

to be questioned. Early on, tree preservation was the corner-stone of park policy, so natural wildfires were squelched whenever possible. But after a noticeable decline in tree germination, research determined that fire is necessary—it dries out the cones to release their seeds, burns underbrush, and clears openings in the canopy for sunlight to reach the seedlings. In 1968, an unprecedented fire-management program began that allows some natural wildfires to burn, sets prescribed burns, and suppresses unwanted blazes. Consequently, the increase in the regeneration rate of giant sequoias has been noticeable.

Other environmental concerns for the park include air quality and drought. Unfortunately, Sequoia & Kings Canyon is located near California's smoggy Central Valley, and thus has the most chronically polluted air of the parks in the American West, often obscuring what would otherwise be superlative views. Consequently, the Environmental Protection Agency designated Sequoia & Kings Canyon as an area in which ozone pollution was a risk to human health. Ozone pollution also weakens the trees so that, when natural drought comes along, these damaged trees often die.

Dealing with the issues facing Yosemite and Sequoia & Kings Canyon requires time, money, and commitment—all high hurdles. Partnerships have been formed with foundations, nature conservancies, and even oil companies to provide funding for study and restoration. But the single biggest issue for both parks remains overcrowding—they are too popular for their own good.

For most of the 20th century and into the 21st, the parks have walked a tenuous line between increasing visitation and consistent management of visitation. Research has changed some policies; experience is changing others; and educational efforts will, we hope, help preserve the parks for future generations of nature enthusiasts.

PLANNING YOUR TRIP TO YOSEMITE AND SEQUOIA & KINGS CANYON NATIONAL PARKS

Visiting California's golden trio of national parks is easy—all are accessible by car. But planning a successful trip can be tricky, especially if you want to explore Yosemite. As one of the nation's favorite parks, it receives more than four million visitors annually. Summer visits are especially difficult: Most park campsites must be reserved months in advance, and lodges may be fully booked as much as a year ahead. The earlier you plan, the better.

GETTING THERE & GETTING AROUND

Getting to Yosemite National Park

BY PLANE

Fresno Yosemite International Airport (www. flyfresno.com; ⓒ **559/621-4500**), located 90 miles from Yosemite National Park's South Entrance at Wawona, is the nearest major airport, serving 13 metropolitan cities daily. Airlines include

Aeromexico (www.aeromexico.com), **Alaska Airlines** (www.alaskaair.com), **Allegiant Air** (www.allegiantair.com), **American Airlines** (www.aa.com), **Frontier Airlines** (flyfrontier.com), **Delta Air Lines** (delta.com), **United Airlines** (www.united.com), and **Volaris** (www.volaris.com).

BY CAR

Yosemite is a 3½-hour drive from San Francisco and a 6-hour drive from Los Angeles. From the Bay Area, the quickest route is CA 120 to the Big Oak Flat entrance, 88 miles from Manteca. From other parts of Northern California, visitors use CA 140 to the Arch Rock entrance, 75 miles northeast of Merced. From Southern California, use CA 41 north of Fresno to the South Entrance. From the east, the Tioga Pass Entrance is 10 miles west of Lee Vining via CA 120. This route is usually open only in summer. Check road conditions at ✆ **800/427-7623** or visit www.dot.ca.gov.

Most major car-rental companies can be found in Fresno, including **Alamo** (www.alamo.com), **Avis** (www.avis.com), **Budget** (www.budget.com), **Dollar** (www.dollar.com), **Enterprise** (www.enterprise.com), **Hertz** (www.hertz.com), and **National** (www.nationalcar.com).

RV rentals are available in Fresno; low-season rates are about $200 a night and high season about $425. Contact "A" Class RV, www.aclassrv.com, or Cruse America, www.cruiseamerica.com.

Note: Insurance and taxes are rarely included in quoted rental-car rates in the U.S. Be sure to ask about additional fees.

BY BUS

Daily bus transportation into the park from Merced, Mariposa, and other nearby communities is provided by the **Yosemite Area Regional Transportation System,** or **YARTS** (yarts.com; ✆ **877/989-2787** or 209/388-9589). Ride the bus and avoid traffic hassles: YARTS buses are not subject to park entrance delays during peak season. Pickups are in Merced, Fresno, Sonora, and Mammoth Lakes. The Merced bus route runs year-round, with 18 stops along the route in Merced, Mariposa, El Portal, and Yosemite. Round-trip fares range from $10 to $30 for adults; reduced fares for seniors, children, and the disabled. Rates include park admission. YARTS connects with other local and intercity transit services such as Greyhound and Amtrak to give riders easy access to the park. In Yosemite, it connects to the park's free shuttle service.

Greyhound (www.greyhound.com; © **800/231-2222**) also links Fresno and Merced with Yosemite National Park, $25 one way.

BY TRAIN
Amtrak (www.amtrak.com; © **800/872-7245**) serves Fresno and Merced on its San Joaquin route and connects Visalia with the Hanford station via bus service.

Getting to Sequoia & Kings Canyon National Parks
BY PLANE
Fresno Yosemite International Airport (www.flyfresno. com; © **559/621-4500**) is the nearest major airport, located 53 miles from the Big Stump Entrance of Kings Canyon. See the section on Yosemite, above, to find out which airlines service Fresno.

BY CAR
There are two entrances to the parks: CA 198 east, via Visalia and the town of Three Rivers, leads to the Ash Mountain Entrance in Sequoia National Park, while CA 180 east, via Fresno, leads to the Big Stump Entrance near Grant Grove in Kings Canyon National Park. Both entrances are approximately 4 hours from Los Angeles and 5 hours from San Francisco. To check on statewide road conditions, call © **800/427-7623** or visit www.dot.ca.gov. For rental-car and RV rental information, see the section on Yosemite, above.

BY BUS
Greyhound (© **800/231-2222**) serves Merced, Visalia, and Fresno. From Visalia, take the **Sequoia Shuttle** (www. sequoiashuttle.com; © **877/287-4453**), to the Giant Forest area of Sequoia. The shuttle runs in the summer and costs $20 roundtrip.

BY TRAIN
Amtrak (www.amtrak.com; © **800/872-7245**) serves Fresno and Merced on its San Joaquin route and connects Visalia with the Hanford station via bus service.

Getting Around Yosemite and Sequoia & Kings Canyon

BY CAR

The most popular way to visit the parks is by car, but traffic can be extremely congested, especially during the summer. Try to be inside the parks by 9am to find parking. Gridlock is at its worst around 3 or 4pm. If you're planning to visit all three parks, you'll probably need a car because of the distances involved.

BY BUS

Daily bus transportation into Yosemite is provided by the **Yosemite Area Regional Transportation System,** or **YARTS** (www.yarts.com; ℡ **877/989-2787**). Buses are not subject to park entrance delays during peak season.

Within Yosemite National Park, the **Yosemite Valley Shuttle** (www.nps.gov) provides free service around eastern Yosemite Valley, including stops at or near all overnight accommodations, stores, and major vistas. In winter there is

---

tips **ON ACCOMMODATIONS**

Your options are limited in the parks; the finite number of rooms and seemingly limitless number of peak-season visitors make for high occupancy and rates. And the fact that many of the parks' lodges have historic designations means they might not fit some visitors' modern tastes.

For information on much of the lodging within Yosemite National Park, contact Aramark, the primary concessionaire (www. travelyosemite.com; ℡ **888/413-8869**). For lodging information and reservations in Sequoia & Kings Canyon, **contact DNC Parks & Resorts,** the primary concessionaire (www.travel yosemite.com; ℡ **877/430-0944** or 801/559-4930). Reservations also can be made for Wuksachi Lodge in the Giant Forest area of Sequoia National Park at ℡ **559/625-7700.** Kings Canyon accommodations, including Grant Grove Village, John Muir Lodge and Cedar Grove Village, can be reserved at ℡ **888/252-5757** or www.visitsequoia.com.

There is more variety in the gateway cities, from dorm-style hostels to high-end resorts. Vacation rentals and house-swapping is a possibility in many of the gateway cities, especially Visalia and Oakhurst.

service to Badger Pass ski area. For a fee, there are also guided tours to Glacier Point and other areas, and a hikers' bus to Tuolumne Meadows (www.travelyosemite.com).

In Sequoia & Kings Canyon, the **Sequoia Shuttle** (www. sequoiashuttle.com; © **877/287-4453**) connects Visalia with the Giant Forest area; it runs in summer for $20 per person round-trip. A free in-park shuttle takes visitors from Giant Forest to Lodgepole, Moro Rock, and other destinations.

SPECIAL PERMITS & PASSES

American parks and monuments are some of the biggest travel bargains in the world. If you plan to visit several national parks and monuments within a year, buy an **America the Beautiful—National Parks & Federal Recreational Lands Annual Pass** for $80 (good for 365 days from the date of purchase at nearly all federal preserves).

Anyone age 62 or older can get a lifetime **Interagency Senior Pass** for a one-time fee of $80 or an annual pass for $20, and people who are blind or who have permanent disabilities can obtain an **Interagency Access Pass,** which costs nothing.

All passes are available at any park entrance point or visitor center. While the Interagency Senior and Interagency Access passes must be purchased in person (to verify age or disability), Interagency Annual Passes are also available online at **shop.usparkpass.com**.

You'll need a **backcountry permit** to camp overnight in the wilderness sections of these parks, but a backcountry permit is not required for day hikes. Reserving an overnight permit costs $5, plus an additional $5 per person in Yosemite National Park (www.yosemiteconservancy.org) and $10 per group plus $5 per person in Sequoia & Kings Canyon national parks. Permits can be reserved up to 24 weeks in advance in Yosemite; it's a good idea to reserve early in the high season. But last-minute permits can sometimes be obtained at permit stations within the parks. In Sequoia & Kings Canyon, availability is limited during the high season from late May to late September. More information is available online at **www.nps.gov/yose** for Yosemite or **www. nps.gov/seki** for Sequoia & Kings Canyon.

Elsewhere in the parks, the usual permits and regulations apply. All anglers 16 and over must have valid California fishing licenses.

PLANNING A BACKCOUNTRY TRIP

While you can find more detailed information for Yosemite and Sequoia & Kings Canyon in their respective chapters, the following are some general things to keep in mind when planning a backcountry trip.

Regulations

The theme in the backcountry is "leave no trace," and that means packing out any garbage you take in, not bringing pets, staying on designated trails, and reusing existing designated campsites so you don't leave scars on the landscape. Maximum party size is 15 for an overnight trip, 25 for a day hike. Fires are allowed only in established fire rings, and only dead and downed material may be used for firewood. Fires are prohibited in some areas. You must have a park permit for overnight stays in the backcountry. For more information on "leave no trace" ethics, see **www.lnt.org**.

Personal Safety Issues

It's best not to backpack alone, but if you must, be sure that you have told both park rangers and friends where you'll be and how long you'll be gone. Don't leave the parking lot without the following gear: a compass, topographical maps, a first-aid kit, bug repellent, toilet paper and a trowel of some sort, a flashlight, matches, a knife, a rope for hanging food supplies in a tree, and a bell or other noisemaker that hopefully will alert any bears in the neighborhood to your presence, as well as a tent, a stove, and a sleeping bag. At this altitude, sunscreen and sunglasses with UV protection are a wise addition. Bear repellent spray, generically referred to as "pepper spray," is available in most sporting-goods stores and has proven successful in countering bear attacks. You'll also need iodine pills or a water filter because that seemingly clear stream is filled with parasites that are likely to cause intestinal disorders. If you don't have iodine or a filter, boil water for at least 5 minutes before you drink it.

Be prepared for sudden changes in weather conditions. Heavy thunderstorms can form in a matter of hours and snow can fall at any time of the year. Summer storms often bring intense rain, hail, and lightning strikes, particularly in mid to late afternoon. During a storm, stay away from peaks, ridges, caves, water, and open areas. Avoid tall, solitary trees.

[FastFACTS] YOSEMITE AND SEQUOIA & KINGS CANYON NATIONAL PARKS

Area Codes The area code for the Yosemite area is **209.** The area code in and around Sequoia & Kings Canyon is **559.**

Business Hours Stores are typically open from 8 or 9am until 7 or 8pm. Banks are generally open from 8 or 9am until 5 or 6pm.

Disabled Travelers People visit these parks to enjoy their scenic beauty, and that can be done in a host of different ways—you don't have to hike 5 miles or climb to the top of a waterfall. Some of the most rewarding moments

come from quiet, still observation.

Be sure to inquire about the National Park Service's free **Interagency Access Pass,** available to the blind and those with permanent disabilities.

In Yosemite, there are some fairly level paved trails around the valley floor, including the ones to Mirror Lake and Happy Isles, and a paved bike trail is also accessible to wheelchairs (see "Bicycling," p. 61). Ask for information on accessible points when making reservations. An accessibility brochure is available at

park entrances and visitor centers, and a park accessibility guide can be found at www.nps.gov/yose/planyourvisit/upload/access.pdf.

In Sequoia & Kings Canyon, all visitor centers and museums have paved, flat paths leading from parking areas to information desks, exhibits, bookstores, water-bottle filling stations, and restrooms. Cedar Grove Visitor Center is small and may be difficult for people in wheelchairs to navigate. Mineral King Ranger Station has steps leading to the entrance and may not be accessible to people with mobility impairments.

Wheelchairs may be borrowed at no cost at Lodgepole Visitor Center and Giant Forest Museum. They can be used anywhere in the parks but must be returned by the end of the day, before each visitor center closes. Special requests should be directed to ⓒ **559/565-3134.**

Doctors In Yosemite National Park, the **Yosemite Medical Clinic** (ⓒ **209/372-4637**) in Yosemite Village is open daily in summer and Monday through Friday the rest of the year. In Sequoia & Kings Canyon, the closest medical facilities are in the gateway towns of Fresno, Visalia, and Three Rivers.

Drinking Laws The legal age for purchase and consumption of alcoholic beverages in the U.S. is 21; proof of age is required and often requested at bars, nightclubs, and restaurants, so it's always a good idea to bring ID when you go out. Do not carry open containers of alcohol in your car or any public area that isn't zoned for alcohol consumption. The police can fine you on the spot. Don't even think about driving while intoxicated. Beer, wine, and liquor are widely available at businesses inside and outside of the parks, and bars stay open as late as 2am.

Electricity Like Canada, the United States uses 110 to 120 volts AC (60 cycles), compared to 220 to 240 volts AC (50 cycles) in most of Europe, Australia, and New Zealand. Downward converters that change 220–240 volts to 110–120 volts are difficult to find in the United States, so bring one with you.

Embassies & Consulates All embassies are in the nation's capital, Washington, DC. Some consulates are in major U.S. cities, and most nations have a mission to the United Nations in New York City. If your country isn't listed below, call for directory information in Washington, DC (ⓒ **202/555-1212**), or check www.embassy.org/embassies.

The embassy of **Australia** is at 1601 Massachusetts Ave. NW, Washington, DC 20036 (www.usa.embassy.gov.au; ⓒ **202/797-3000**). Consulates are in New York, Honolulu, Houston, Los Angeles, and San Francisco.

The embassy of **Canada** is at 501 Pennsylvania Ave. NW, Washington, DC 20001 (www.canadainternational.gc.ca/washington; ⓒ **202/682-1740**). Other Canadian consulates are in Buffalo (New York), Detroit, Los Angeles, New York, and Seattle.

The embassy of **Ireland** is at 2234 Massachusetts Ave. NW, Washington, DC 20008 (www.embassyofireland.org; ⓒ **202/462-3939**). Irish consulates are in Boston, Chicago, New York, San Francisco, and other cities. See website for complete listing.

The embassy of **New Zealand** is at 37 Observatory Circle NW, Washington, DC 20008 (www.nzembassy.com; ⓒ **202/328-4800**). New Zealand consulates are in Los Angeles, Salt Lake City, San Francisco, and Seattle.

The embassy of the **United Kingdom** is at 3100 Massachusetts Ave. NW, Washington, DC 20008 (http://ukinusa.fco.gov.uk; ℂ **202/588-6500**). Other British consulates are in Atlanta, Boston, Chicago, Cleveland, Houston, Los Angeles, New York, San Francisco, and Seattle.

Emergencies Call ℂ **911.**

Family Travel

Yosemite schedules a variety of children's programs. Kids ages 3 to 6 can join the **Little Cubs,** and those from 7 to 13 can become **Junior Rangers,** by completing projects in a booklet ($3 for Little Cubs and $3.50 for Junior Rangers); those in the Junior Ranger program also collect a bag of trash and participate in a ranger program. Upon completion, Little Cubs receive a button; Junior Rangers get a patch. The booklets are available at the Nature Center at Happy Isles, Yosemite Valley and Tuolumne Meadows visitor centers, and the Wawona and Big Oak Flat information stations.

Free ranger-led walks and talks, many suitable for kids, are held at various locations throughout the park. The programs vary by season, so check your *Yosemite Guide* (handed out at park entrances) to find out what's happening during your visit.

The **Happy Isles Nature Center** (shuttle bus stop no. 16) teaches about the fauna and eco-systems of the park. It has interactive displays and dioramas of park animals that children will enjoy. It is visited annually by more than 10,000 families.

During the summer, Sequoia & Kings Canyon offer ranger-led walks aimed at families, as well as a campfire program at Lodgepole (check at visitor centers for the current schedule). In addition, the parks have a Junior Ranger program like Yosemite's, in which children get booklets and complete various activities to become Junior Rangers. Another child-friendly option is the **Beetle Rock Education Center** near the Giant Forest Museum, open on summer weekends only.

Health Health hazards range from mild headaches to run-ins with wild animals, but the latter happen less frequently than car accidents in the parks. To be on the safe side, you might want to keep a **first-aid kit** in your car or luggage and have it handy when hiking.

The most common health hazard is the discomfort felt as visitors adjust to the parks' high elevations. **Altitude sickness** is a process that can take a day or more. Symptoms include headache, fatigue, nausea, loss of appetite, muscle pain, and lightheadedness. Doctors recommend that, until acclimated, travelers should avoid heavy exertion, consume light meals, and drink lots of liquids, avoiding those with caffeine or alcohol.

Wildlife are to be treated with utmost respect in the parks, for your health's sake and theirs. Keep your distance—at least 100 yards if possible—from any wild animal, including small rodents such as squirrels, which can spread the plague and other diseases. And don't tempt fate by taking selfies in dangerous conditions. Three people were swept over 317-foot Vernal

Fall after climbing over a guard rail to snap photos.

Two **waterborne hazards** are *Giardia* and *campylobacter*, with symptoms that wreak havoc on the human digestive system. Untreated water from the parks' lakes and streams should be boiled for at least 5 minutes before consumption, treated with iodine pills, or pumped through a fine-mesh water filter specifically designed to remove bacteria.

Internet & Wi-Fi Internet access and Wi-Fi are available free to the public at two locations, the Mariposa County library branch in Yosemite Valley (Girl's Club on Village Drive), and at Degnan's Kitchen. Internet access is available to registered guests at The Majestic Yosemite Hotel (formerly The Ahwahnee), Yosemite Valley Lodge (formerly Yosemite Lodge), Half Dome Village (formerly Curry Village), and Big Trees Lodge (formerly Wawona hotel).

Legal Aid While driving, if you are pulled over for a minor infraction (such as speeding), never attempt to pay the fine directly to a police officer; this could be construed as attempted bribery, a much more serious crime. Pay fines by mail or directly into the hands of the clerk of the court. If accused of a more serious offense, say and do nothing before consulting a lawyer. In the U.S., the burden is on the state to prove a person's guilt beyond a reasonable doubt, and everyone has the right to remain silent, whether he or she is suspected of a crime or actually arrested. Once arrested, a person can make one telephone call to a party of his or her choice. The international visitor should call his or her embassy or consulate.

LGBTQ-Friendly Travel The parks are generally gay-friendly. San Francisco, a gateway to the parks, is a magnet for LGBTQ travelers. But gay culture and nightlife are limited in the small towns near the parks.

Mail At press time, domestic postage rates were 35¢ for a postcard and 55¢ for a letter. For international mail, a first-class letter of up to 1 ounce costs $1.15; a first-class postcard costs the same as a letter. For more information, go to **www. usps.com**.

If you aren't sure what your address will be in the United States, mail can be sent to you, in your name, c/o General Delivery at the main post office of the city or region where you expect to be. (Call ℂ **800/275-8777** for information on the nearest post office.) The addressee must pick up mail in person and must produce proof of identity (driver's license, passport, and the like). Most post offices will hold mail for up to 1 month and are open Monday to Friday from 8am to 6pm, and Saturday from 9am to 3pm.

Medical Requirements Unless you're arriving from an area known to be suffering from an epidemic (particularly cholera or yellow fever), inoculations or vaccinations are not required for entry into the United States.

Mobile Phones

Cell service is widely available on the floor of Yosemite Valley and parts of Tuolumne Meadows; in Sequoia & Kings Canyon, it is available in the villages but largely unavailable on the roads and in wilderness areas. Cell service is available in all gateway cities, but the signal can be weak.

Money & Costs

Frommer's lists exact prices in the local currency. The currency conversions provided were correct at press time. However, rates fluctuate, so before departing, consult a currency exchange website such as **www.oanda.com/currency/converter** to check up-to-the-minute rates.

Yosemite is a premium-priced destination, with lodging and meals priced accordingly high, especially during the summer season. In fall and spring, room rates drop sharply. Sequoia & Kings Canyon are more moderately priced. There are ATMs in most of the developed areas in the parks.

THE VALUE OF THE U.S. DOLLAR VS. OTHER POPULAR CURRENCIES

US$	Aus$	Can$	Euro (€)	NZ$	UK£
$1	A$1.46	C$1.32	€.90	NZ$1.53	£.82

For help with currency conversions, tip calculations, and more, download Frommer's convenient Travel Tools app for your mobile device. Go to **www.frommers.com/go/mobile** and click on the Travel Tools icon.

Packing Prepare yourself for every possible situation: Bring warm- and cold-weather clothing in layers. A jacket is a necessity year-round; it can be considerably warmer in the low country around the parks than in the elevations of the High Sierra. If you are camping or backpacking, good packing is of the essence. For more helpful information on packing for your trip, download our convenient Travel Tools app for your mobile device. Go to **www.frommers.com/go/mobile** and click on the Travel Tools icon.

Passports Virtually every air traveler entering the U.S. is required to show a passport. All persons, including U.S. citizens, traveling by air between the United States and other nations, including Canada, Mexico, Central and South America, the Caribbean, and Bermuda are required to present a valid passport.

Note: U.S. and Canadian citizens entering the U.S. at land and sea ports of entry from within the Western Hemisphere must also present a passport or other documents compliant with the Western Hemisphere Travel Initiative (WHTI; see https://www.cbp.gov/travel/us-citizens/western-hemisphere-travel-initiative for

WHAT THINGS COST IN YOSEMITE AND SEQUOIA & KINGS CANYON (US$)

Admission into the parks for 7 days	35.00
Double room in Yosemite, moderate	150.00–275.00
Double room in Yosemite, expensive	590.00
Cabin in Yosemite	100.00–260.00
Double room in Sequoia & Kings Canyon, moderate	100.00–200.00
Double room in Sequoia & Kings Canyon, expensive	150.00–300.00
Cabin in Sequoia & Kings Canyon	60.00–200.00
Campsite in either park	10.00–30.00
Dinner main course	10.00–35.00
1 gallon of premium gas	4.00

details). Children traveling internationally must also present a passport. For information on obtaining a passport, see the following:

Australian citizens should contact the **Australian Passport Information Service** (www.passports.gov. au; *(C)* **131-232**).

Canadian citizens should contact the **Passport Office,** Department of Foreign Affairs and International Trade, Ottawa, ON K1A 0G3 (www.ppt.gc.ca; *(C)* **800/567-6868**).

Irish citizens should contact the **Passport Office,** Setanta Centre, Molesworth Street, Dublin 2 (www. foreignaffairs.gov.ie; *(C)* **01/671-1633**).

New Zealand citizens should contact the **Passports Office,** Department of International Affairs, 47 Boulcott St., Wellington 6011 (www.passports. govt.nz; *(C)* **0800/225-050** in New Zealand or 04/474-8100).

U.K. citizens should visit the nearest passport office, major post office, or travel agency, or contact the **HM Passport Office,** 89 Eccleston Square, London, SW1V 1PN (www.gov. uk/government/ organisations/hm-passport-office; *(C)* **0300/222-0000**).

U.S. citizens should check the U.S. State Department website (travel.state.gov/passport) or call the **National Passport Information Center** (*(C)* **877/487-2778**) for automated information.

Pet Travel Want to bring Fido along on your park trip? Although traveling with pets is allowed in most national parks, including Yosemite and Sequoia & Kings Canyon, there are restrictions that complicate the matter. Pets are not allowed in any lodging in Yosemite and are not allowed on most trails. However, they are allowed in most campgrounds. In developed areas, such as the Yosemite

Valley, your pet can take a walk with you on paved roads, sidewalks, and bicycle paths. But he must be restrained on a leash not more than 6 feet (1.8 meters) long. Leashed pets cannot be left unattended and, of course, you're expected to clean up after your pet.

A dog kennel is available May through September at Yosemite Valley Stable, but there are restrictions, and reservations are highly recommended (www.travelyosemite. com; ℰ **209/372-8326**). Boarding is also available in gateway cities: Fresno, Merced, and Visalia.

Many of the same restrictions are also in effect at Sequoia & Kings Canyon parks. Pets are not permitted on any trails, they must be leashed in campgrounds and picnic areas, and the leash cannot be longer than 6 feet (1.8 meters) long. Pets cannot be left tied and unattended at any time. They should not be left in hot vehicles.

Remember that pet food is also bear food: Store pet food as if it were human food.

In the national forest lands that surround these parks, leashed pets are allowed on trails.

Police Call ℰ **911.** National Park Service rangers serve as police in the parks, as do county officials.

Safety The following are some general safety tips for visitors to Yosemite and Sequoia & Kings Canyon:

○ Although some of the bridges that cross rivers and streams look inviting, resist the temptation to use them as diving boards—it's not only dangerous, but also illegal.

○ Trails, especially ones over rock and granite, can be slick. Be especially careful along any rivers or creeks, such as Mist Trail in Yosemite, where wind and water can produce treacherous conditions.

○ Always carry more than enough water, especially when going into higher elevations where the body requires more hydration.

○ Under no circumstances should food be left in tents, cabins, or cars. There are storage lockers and bear-proof containers throughout the park—use them.

○ Under no circumstances should you feed a bear—or any wild animal, for that matter.

○ Always carry a map if you go hiking, even for short day hikes. If you have maps on your phone or tablet, be sure to download them for offline use, as cell coverage is unlikely in many hiking areas.

Another note on safety: Nothing will ruin a trip to the parks faster than sore or wet feet. Take some time planning your travel wardrobe. Bring comfortable walking shoes that are broken in, even if you plan to keep walking to a minimum. If you want to do some serious hiking, get sturdy boots that support your ankles and wick away water. Early in the season, trails may be wet or muddy; late in the fall, snowfall is a possibility. The more popular trails are sometimes also used by horses, which can make stream crossings a mucky mess.

Wear clothing in layers and bring a small backpack so that you can take those layers off and on as the temperature, altitude, and your physical exertion change. Cotton is a no-no in the backcountry; synthetic fabrics are recommended because they dry much faster. Gloves or mittens are useful before the park heats up, or in the evening when it cools down again, *even in summer.*

The atmosphere is thin at higher altitudes, so protect your skin. Bring a strong sunblock, a hat with a brim, and sunglasses. Insect repellent, water bottles, and a first-aid kit are also recommended.

Senior Travel

Anyone 62 or older can get a lifetime **Interagency Senior Pass** for a one-time fee of $80. The senior rate for an annual pass is $20. The passes are available at any entrance point to Yosemite or Sequoia & Kings Canyon. The Interagency Senior Pass must be purchased in person in order to verify age.

Smoking Smoking is banned in all public places in the parks and bars and restaurants in the gateway towns. Some establishments offer an outdoor smoking area.

Taxes The United States has no value-added tax (VAT) or other indirect tax at the national level. Every state, county, and city may levy its own local tax on all purchases, including hotel and restaurant checks and airline tickets. These taxes will not appear on price tags. Taxes total around 7% to 11% in the parks and the gateways.

Telephones Many convenience groceries and packaging services sell **prepaid calling cards** in denominations up to $50. **To make calls within the United States and to Canada,** dial 1 followed by the area code and the seven-digit number. **For other international calls,** dial 011 followed by the country code, city code, and the number you are calling.

For **reversed-charge or collect calls,** and for person-to-person calls, dial the number 0, then the area code and number; an operator will come on the line, and you should specify whether you are calling collect, person-to-person, or both. If your operator-assisted call is international, ask for the overseas operator.

For **directory assistance** ("Information"), dial ✆ **411** for local numbers and national numbers in the U.S. and Canada. (A fee may apply.) For dedicated long-distance information, dial 1, then the appropriate area code plus 555-1212.

Time As with all of California, the parks are on **Pacific Standard Time (PST).** When it's 9am in Yosemite (PST), it's noon in New York City (EST) and 5pm in London (GMT).

Daylight saving time (summer time) is in effect from 1am on the second Sunday in March to 1am on the first Sunday in November, except in Arizona, Hawaii, the

U.S. Virgin Islands, and Puerto Rico. Daylight saving time moves the clock 1 hour ahead of standard time. For help with time translations, and more, download our convenient Travel Tools app for your mobile device. Go to **www.frommers.com/go/mobile** and click on the Travel Tools icon.

Tipping   In hotels, tip **bellhops** at least $1 to $2 per bag ($3–$5 if you have a lot of luggage) and tip the **chamber staff** $2 to $3 per day (more if you've left a big mess for him or her to clean up). Tip the **doorman** or **concierge** only if he or she has provided you with some specific service (for example, calling a cab for you or obtaining difficult-to-get theater tickets). Tip the **valet-parking attendant** $2 every time you get your car.

In restaurants, bars, and nightclubs, tip **service staff** and **bartenders** 15% to 20% of the check, tip **checkroom attendants** $1 per garment, and tip **valet-parking attendants** $2 per vehicle.

As for other service personnel, tip **cab drivers** 15% to 20% of the fare, tip **skycaps** at airports at least $2 per bag ($3–$4 if you have a lot of luggage), and tip **hairdressers** and **barbers** 15% to 20%.

For help with tip calculations, currency conversions, and more, download our convenient Travel Tools app for your mobile device. Go to **www.frommers.com/go/mobile** and click on the Travel Tools icon.

Toilets   You won't find public toilets or "restrooms" on the streets in most U.S. cities, but they can be found in hotel lobbies, bars, restaurants, museums, department stores, railway and bus stations, and service stations. Large hotels and fast-food restaurants are often the best bet for clean facilities. There are public restrooms at many pull-offs on the road, in the parks, as well as at all visitor centers and many trail heads.

Visas   The U.S. State Department has a **Visa Waiver Program (VWP)** allowing citizens of the

following countries to enter the United States without a visa for stays of up to 90 days: Andorra, Australia, Austria, Belgium, Brunei, Chile, Czech Republic, Denmark, Estonia, Finland, France, Germany, Greece, Hungary, Iceland, Ireland, Italy, Japan, Latvia, Liechtenstein, Lithuania, Luxembourg, Malta, Monaco, the Netherlands, New Zealand, Norway, Portugal, San Marino, Singapore, Slovakia, Slovenia, South Korea, Spain, Sweden, Switzerland, Taiwan, and the United Kingdom. (This list was accurate at press time; for the most up-to-date list of countries in the VWP, consult http://travel.state.gov/visa.)

Even though a visa isn't necessary, in an effort to help U.S. officials check travelers against terror watch lists before they arrive at U.S. borders, visitors from VWP countries must register online through the Electronic System for Travel Authorization (ESTA) before boarding a plane or a boat to the U.S. Travelers must complete an electronic application providing basic personal and travel eligibility information. The Department of Homeland Security recommends filling out the form at least 3 days before traveling. Authorizations will be valid for up to 2 years or until the traveler's passport expires, whichever comes first. Currently, there is a US$14 fee for the online application. Existing ESTA registrations remain valid through their expiration dates.

Note: Any passport issued on or after April 1, 2016, by a VWP country must be an **e-Passport** for VWP travelers to be eligible to enter the U.S. without a visa. Citizens of these nations also need to present a round-trip air or cruise ticket upon arrival. For more information, go to **http://travel.state.gov/visa**. Canadian citizens may enter the United States without visas but will need to show passports and proof of residence. Citizens of all other countries must have (1) a valid passport that expires at least 6 months later than the scheduled end of

their visit to the U.S.; and (2) a tourist visa.

For information about U.S. visas, go to **http://travel.state.gov** and click on "Visas."

Visitor Information If you're planning a visit to Yosemite National Park, you can get general information on accommodations, weather, and permits from the park's phone menu at ⓒ **209/372-0200** or online at **www.nps.gov/yose**. You can buy books and maps from the nonprofit **Yosemite Conservancy** (www.yosemiteconservancy.org; ⓒ **209/379-2317**). Information on lodging and activities outside the park is available from the visitor centers and chambers of commerce in the park's surrounding cities. If you're coming from the west on CA 120, contact the **Tuolumne County Visitor Center** in Sonora (www.visittuolumne.com; ⓒ **800/446-1333** or 209/533-4420) or the **Yosemite Chamber of Commerce** in Groveland (www.groveland.org; ⓒ **209/962-0429**). On CA 140, contact

the **Mariposa County Visitors Bureau** (www.homeofyosemite.com; ⓒ **866/425-3366** or 209/966-2456). On CA 41, south of the park, call the **Yosemite Sierra Visitors Bureau** in Oakhurst (www.yosemitethisyear.com; ⓒ **559/683-4636**). From Lee Vining on the park's eastern boundary, contact the **Lee Vining Chamber of Commerce** (www.leevining.com; ⓒ **760/647-6629**). There's a **California Welcome Center** in Merced (www.visitmerced.travel; ⓒ **800/446-5353** or 209/724-8104).

In Sequoia & Kings Canyon, start your search at the National Park Service website at **www.nps.gov/seki**, which provides the most up-to-date information on the park, lodging, hikes, regulations, and the best times to visit. Much of the same information, plus road conditions, is available by phone (ⓒ **559/565-3341**).

Water See "Health," p. 175–176.

When to Go During the **high season,** June to August, the parks are crowded, and temperatures are high. In Yosemite Valley and lower areas of Sequoia & Kings Canyon, temperatures often reach 90 degrees (32°C) or more, but you'll cool off as you ascend to higher regions of the parks. All park trails and facilities are usually open during this period. One downside: You'll see less volume in the parks' streams and waterfalls; some may dry up completely. During the parks' **shoulder seasons,** April to May and September to October, there are fewer crowds and temperatures will lessen, but high-country passes and ridges may be inaccessible because of snow. In spring, waterfalls are magnificent and weekday visits are easy, with crowds surging into the parks only on weekends. Fall is also less crowded, and foliage brightens visits during this period. Temperatures usually drop in late October. Snow is always a possibility. During the **low season,** November to March, snow closes many roads. Many facilities shut down. But the parks are open year-round, with accommodations available at lower rates during the winter.

Index

Map List

Photo Credits

p. i: Andrew Opila; p. ii: Phil Vinke; p. iii: My Good Images; p. iv: welcomia; p. v, top: Nikolas_jkd; p. v, bottom: RodClementPhotography; p. vi, top: Roel Slootweg / Shutterstock.com; p. vi, middle: Courtesy of Yosemite Mariposa County Tourism Bureau / Kim Lawson; p. vi, bottom: Sundry Photography / Shutterstock.com; p. vii, top left: Sarah Fields Photography; p. vii, top right: Schuseb; p. vii, bottom: Courtesy of Yosemite Mariposa County Tourism Bureau; p. viii, top: Sierralara; p. viii, bottom: PR Image Factory; p. ix, top: Celso Diniz; p. ix, middle: Sean R. Stubben; p. ix, bottom: Sean R. Stubben; p. x, top: Courtesy of Yosemite Mariposa County Tourism Bureau; p. x, middle: Courtesy of Yosemite Mariposa County Tourism Bureau / Kenny Karst; p. x, bottom: Courtesy of Yosemite Mariposa County Tourism Bureau; p. xi, top left: My Good Images; p. xi, top right: Phil Vinke; p. xi, bottom: NatalieJean; p. xii, top: Oscity; p. xii, middle: travelview / Shutterstock.com; p. xii, bottom: Courtesy of NPS Photo; p. xiii, top left: Oscity; p. xiii, top right: NatalieJean; p. xiii, bottom: National Parked; p. xiv, top: Phil Vinke; p. xiv, middle: Courtesy of Montecito Sequoia Lodge; p. xiv, bottom: Kara Jade Quan-Montgomery; p. xv, top: Courtesy of NPS Photo; p. xv, middle: Bryan Brazil; p. xv, bottom: Margaret.W; p. xvi, top left: Tom Grundy; p. xvi, top right: weltreisendertj; p. xvi, bottom left: Margaret.W; p. xvi, bottom right: Tom Grundy.

Frommer's Yosemite & Neighboring Parks, 9th edition

Published by
FROMMER MEDIA LLC

ISBN 978-1-62887-480-8 (paper), 978-1-62887-481-5 (ebk)

Editorial Director: Pauline Frommer
Editor: Elizabeth Heath
Production Editor: Erin Geile
Cartographer: Roberta Stockwell
Photo Editor: Meghan Lamb
Assistant Photo Editor and Contributing Photographer: Phil Vinke
Cover Design: Dave Riedy

Front cover photo: Cathedral Beach in Yosemite Valley; credit: Invisible Witness / Shutterstock.com.

Back cover photo: Walking among giants, Sequoia National Park; credit: Jeison Jaramillo / Shutterstock.

For information on our other products or services, see www.frommers.com.

FrommerMedia LLC also publishes its books in a variety of electronic formats. Some content that appears in print may not be available in electronic formats.

Manufactured in the United States of America

5 4 3 2 1

ABOUT THE AUTHORS

California native **Rosemary McClure** likes to say she was born with a suitcase in her hand. A longtime travel writer for the *Los Angeles Times*, she loves sharing her worldwide finds with others. One of her favorite destinations, however, isn't far from her Long Beach, California home—Yosemite, Sequoia & Kings Canyon National Parks—a majestic mountain loop that offers spectacular waterfalls, deep canyons, vast caverns, and the world's largest trees.

Photojournalist and writer **Jim Edwards** has been published in newspapers and magazines such as the *Washington Post*, *New York Times*, and *Sports Illustrated* for more than 25 years. The Riverside, California resident first visited the great national parks of his California in the 1970s, and has since enjoyed America's "best idea" from coast to coast.

ABOUT THE FROMMER TRAVEL GUIDES

For most of the past 50 years, Frommer's has been the leading series of travel guides in North America, accounting for as many as 24% of all guidebooks sold. I think I know why.

Though we hope our books are entertaining, we nevertheless deal with travel in a serious fashion. Our guidebooks have never looked on such journeys as a mere recreation, but as a far more important human function, a time of learning and introspection, an essential part of a civilized life. We stress the culture, lifestyle, history, and beliefs of the destinations we cover, and urge our readers to seek out people and new ideas as the chief rewards of travel.

We have never shied from controversy. We have, from the beginning, encouraged our authors to be intensely judgmental, critical—both pro and con—in their comments, and wholly independent. Our only clients are our readers, and we have triggered the ire of countless prominent sorts, from a tourist newspaper we called "practically worthless" (it unsuccessfully sued us) to the many rip-offs we've condemned.

And because we believe that travel should be available to everyone regardless of their incomes, we have always been cost-conscious at every level of expenditure. Though we have broadened our recommendations beyond the budget category, we insist that every lodging we include be sensibly priced. We use every form of media to assist our readers, and are particularly proud of our feisty daily website, the award-winning Frommers.com.

I have high hopes for the future of Frommer's. May these guidebooks, in all the years ahead, continue to reflect the joy of travel and the freedom that travel represents. May they always pursue a cost-conscious path, so that people of all incomes can enjoy the rewards of travel. And may they create, for both the traveler and the persons among whom we travel, a community of friends, where all human beings live in harmony and peace.

Arthur Frommer